W9-CUN-707

Critical & Creative Thinking Activities

Grade 3

Author: Rachel Lynette
Editor: Marilyn Evans
Copy Editing: Carrie Gwynne
Art Direction: Cheryl Puckett
Cover Illustration: Nathan Jarvis
Illustration: Jo Larsen
Design/Production: Yuki Meyer

EMC 3393

Evan-Moor®
EDUCATIONAL PUBLISHERS
Helping Children Learn since 1979

Visit
teaching-standards.com
to view a correlation
of this book.
This is a free service.

***Correlated to State and
Common Core State Standards***

**Congratulations on your purchase of some of the
finest teaching materials in the world.**

*Photocopying the pages in this book
is permitted for <u>single-classroom use only</u>.
Making photocopies for additional classes
or schools is prohibited.*

For information about other Evan-Moor products, call 1-800-777-4362,
fax 1-800-777-4332, or visit our Web site, www.evan-moor.com.
Entire contents © 2009 EVAN-MOOR CORP.
18 Lower Ragsdale Drive, Monterey, CA 93940-5746. Printed in USA.

CONTENTS

What's in This Book?........ 4

Through the Year

Spectacular September 5

October Chills 8

Feasting in November 11

December Celebrations........... 14

January Is #1 17

February Fun 20

Marvelous March 23

April Surprises 26

Hey, It's May! 29

Jazzed About June................ 32

Animals

Monkeys........................ 35

Spiders.......................... 38

Ribbit! 41

Pets............................. 44

Reptiles 47

Quack! 50

Slugs and Worms................. 53

Bzzzzzzzz 56

Lions, Tigers, and Bears 59

Ocean Life 62

Places

Home Sweet Home 65

In Our Classroom 68

In the Woods 71

At a Party 74

In the Garden.................... 77

Time to Eat

Pizza Time...................... 80

Lunchtime 83

Eat Your Veggies 86

All About Apples................. 89

I Scream for Ice Cream 92

Things I Use

All Wet 95

What I Wear..................... 98

Boxes........................... 101

Pockets 104

Bottles and Jars 107

Paper........................... 110

In My World

Cartoons......................... 113

Listen!.......................... 116

On the Screen 119

Lost and Found 122

Giggles 125

Nighttime....................... 128

My Birthday 131

Homework 134

Books........................... 137

Cents Sense 140

Answer Key 143

What's in This Book?

Critical and Creative Thinking Activities, Grade 3 contains 46 themes, each presented in a three-page unit that gives students valuable practice with a broad range of thinking skills. The engaging themes will keep students interested and will have them begging to do the next set of activities!

The first and second pages of each unit get students thinking about the topic in a variety of ways. They may be asked to draw on prior knowledge or to generate new ideas.

The last page of each unit features one of a number of stimulating and entertaining formats, including logic puzzles, riddles, and secret codes.

How to Use This Book

• Use the activity pages during your language arts period to keep the rest of the class actively and productively engaged while you work with small groups of students.

• The themed sets of activity pages provide a perfect language arts supplement for your thematic or seasonal units. And you'll find any number of topics that complement your science and social studies curricula.

• Your students will enjoy doing these fun pages for homework or as free-time activities in class.

About the Correlations for This Book

The valuable thinking skills practiced in this book (see inside front cover) are not generally addressed in state standards. However, thinking skills require content to be practiced. The activities in this book have been correlated to the Language Arts and Mathematics standards.

Visit www.teaching-standards.com to view a correlation of this book to your state's standards.

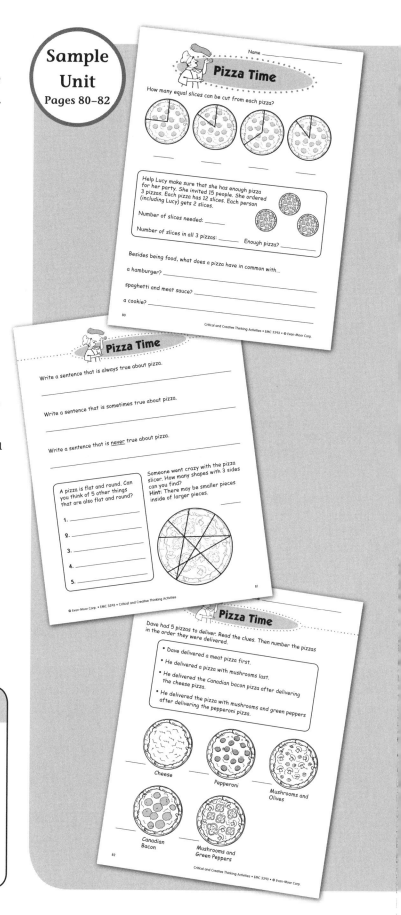

Sample Unit
Pages 80–82

Name _____

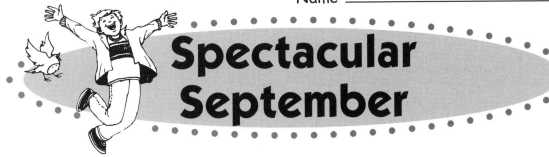

Spectacular September

What is the best thing about starting school again?

_____

What is the hardest thing about starting school again?

_____

Krystal catches the bus at 8:30. It takes her 10 minutes to walk to the bus stop, 5 minutes to get her school stuff together, 15 minutes to eat breakfast, and 25 minutes to bathe and get dressed. At what time does Krystal need to get up?

_____

At what time do you get up for school?

_____

Do you get up earlier or later than Krystal?

_____

How much earlier or later do you get up?

_____

Unscramble the words to make a sentence.

day   autumn   the   September   in   first   of   is

_____

Spectacular September

Write a sentence using the words **September**, **school**, and **summer**.

_____

_____

Write a sentence about September. Use exactly 6 words.

_____

What are 5 things that you <u>must</u> have on the first day of school?

1. _____

2. _____

3. _____

4. _____

5. _____

Write the word **September** in this **S** so that it fills most of the space.

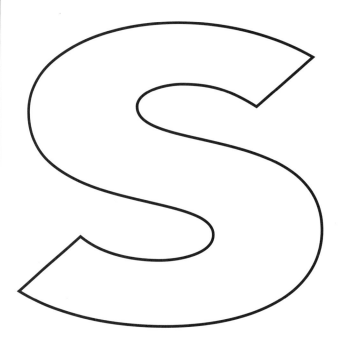

What is another 9-letter word that begins with **S**?

___ ___ ___ ___ ___ ___ ___ ___ ___

 Critical and Creative Thinking Activities • EMC 3393 • © Evan-Moor Corp.

Spectacular September

Oh dear, it is only the first day of school, and Alex has already forgotten something important! For each clue, find the letter that is in the first boldfaced word but <u>not</u> in the second boldfaced word. Then write the letters in order on the lines at the bottom of this page to find out what Alex forgot.

- It is in **CATCH** but not in **CACTUS**.

- It is in **KITE** but not in **TAKE**.

- It is in **CHEST** but not in **CHEAT**.

- It is in **SLIP** but not in **PIES**.

- It is in **PLUS** but not in **SLAP**.

- It is in **NICE** but not in **CITIES**.

- It is in **RICE** but not in **RIGHT**.

- It is in **HARP** but not in **PARTY**.

What can Alex do to solve his problem?

_____

_____

_____

_____

_____

Alex forgot

___ ___ ___ ___ ___ ___ ___ ___ ___ .

© Evan-Moor Corp. • EMC 3393 • Critical and Creative Thinking Activities

October Chills

Draw the other half of the jack-o'-lantern.

What are the 3 scariest costumes that you can think of?

1. _____

2. _____

3. _____

Both **trick** and **treat** begin with **tr**. Read the clues to complete these other **tr** words.

All aboard!   t r ____ ____ ____

Elephant's   t r ____ ____ ____

Pine or oak   t r ____ ____

Hike here   t r ____ ____ ____

It's a fact.   t r ____ ____

3 wheels   t r ____ ____ ____

Analogies

Halloween is to **October** as **Thanksgiving** is to _____.

Candy is to **Halloween** as **presents** are to _____.

Pumpkin is to **orange** as **bat** is to _____.

October Chills

What is your favorite Halloween treat? _____

Owen wants to be a pirate for Halloween. What will he need for his costume?

_____

_____

_____

_____

_____

Riley wants to be a witch for Halloween. What will she need for her costume?

_____

_____

_____

_____

_____

Write **R** if you think the Halloween creature is **real**. Write **N** if you think it is **not real**.

_____ black cat   _____ spider   _____ pirate

_____ werewolf   _____ wizard   _____ alien

_____ ghost   _____ vampire   _____ fairy

© Evan-Moor Corp. • EMC 3393 • Critical and Creative Thinking Activities

October Chills

Use the recipe to fill in the missing amounts below.

Witches' Brew (serves 2)

Make a fire. In a large cauldron, mix:

    7 gerbils' tails   **1 Twinkie**

    $1\frac{1}{2}$ frogs   **26 crickets' legs**

    $2\frac{1}{3}$ cups sour milk   **$\frac{1}{3}$ cup eyeballs**

Stir over the fire for two days. Serve hot.

Fill in the amounts to make Witches' Brew for 4 people.

_____ gerbils' tails   _____ Twinkies

_____ frogs   _____ crickets' legs

_____ cups sour milk   _____ cup(s) eyeballs

Fill in the amounts to make Witches' Brew for 6 people.

_____ gerbils' tails   _____ Twinkies

_____ frogs   _____ crickets' legs

_____ cups sour milk   _____ cup(s) eyeballs

 Critical and Creative Thinking Activities • EMC 3393 • © Evan-Moor Corp.

Name _____

Feasting in November

these things
6. The thing
most thankful
d be number 1.

___ food

___ friends

___ toys

___ education

___ family

___ video games

You are making Thanksgiving dinner, but you <u>cannot</u> make turkey, mashed potatoes, or any of the usual Thanksgiving Day foods. What will you make?

_____

_____

_____

_____

_____

iving is always on the 4th Thursday in November.
ch clue about another holiday, and then write its name.

t day of the tenth month _____

h day of the seventh month _____

th of a month that begins with **M** _____

th of a month that begins with **F** _____

Critical and Creative Thinking Activities • EMC 3393 • © Evan-Moor Corp.

Feasting in November

The answer is **November**. What is the question?

_____

The answer is **Thanksgiving**. What is the question?

_____

Nun
fron
you
for s

A turkey needs to be cooked for 20 minutes a pound. How long should each of these turkeys be cooked?

5 pounds = _____ hours _____ minutes

8 pounds = _____ hours _____ minutes

14 pounds = _____ hours _____ minutes

17 pounds = _____ hours _____ minutes

20 pounds = _____ hours _____ minutes

What Thanks
begins with e
letters?

T_____

P_____

C_____

G_____

S_____

Thank
Read

• the

• the

• the 1

• the 1

What is your favorite Thanksgiving Day food?

_____

Feasting in November

You are having Thanksgiving dinner at your house! There will be 18 guests! You have 4 small tables and 2 big tables. The small tables can fit 4 people, one person on each side. The big tables can fit 6 people, 2 on each side and 1 person on each end. Arrange the tables so that every table is used, everyone has a seat, and there are no empty spaces. The tables may or may not be pushed together.

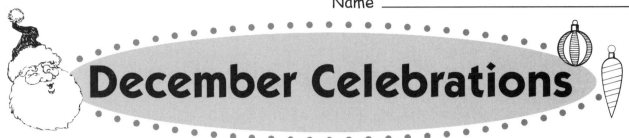

December Celebrations

What do you want for Christmas or Hanukkah that does <u>not</u> need batteries and that does <u>not</u> have an electrical plug?

_____

Tony has a string of 50 Christmas lights. Every 6th light is blue. How many blue lights are there on the string?

_____ blue lights

David got 1 quarter on the first day of Hanukkah. He got 2 quarters on the second day, 3 on the third day, and so on, through the last day of Hanukkah. How many quarters did David get in all 8 days?

_____ quarters

How much money is that?

$_____

Write the letter or letters shared by the shapes.

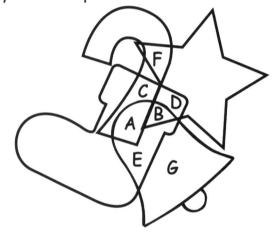

candy cane and stocking _____

bell and stocking _____

star, bell, and stocking _____

candy cane, bell, and stocking _____

just 1 shape _____

December Celebrations

Describe Christmas or Hanukkah in 1 sentence. _____

_____

Circle 5 things that you would <u>most</u> like to find in your stocking.

candy cane   comic book

bouncy ball   card game

stuffed animal   socks

chocolate Santa   yo-yo

spinning top   mittens

Add 2 more to the list.

Frosty the Snowman

Silent Night

Santa Claus Is Coming to Town

_____

_____

If you could give the same gift to every child in the world, what would you give?

_____

Why? _____

December Celebrations

Color the grid to find the hidden picture.

	1	2	3	4	5	6	7	8	9
A									
B									
C									
D									
E									
F									
G									
H									
I									

F5 = green

G9, H9 = green

E4 = red

H1 = green

H6 = green

A5 = yellow

F2–F4 = green

H8 = green

E8, F8, G8 = green

G5 = yellow

E2, E3 = green

C5, C6 = green

B4–B6 = green

C7, D7 = green

I5 = brown

G3, G4 = green

D4, D5 = green

G7 = red

H2 = green

F6, G6 = green

E4 = red

E7 = blue

H7 = green

H3–H5 = green

D3 = green

G2 = blue

F7 = green

C3 = green

G1 = green

D6 = yellow

C4 = blue

E5, E6 = green

Critical and Creative Thinking Activities • EMC 3393 • © Evan-Moor Corp.

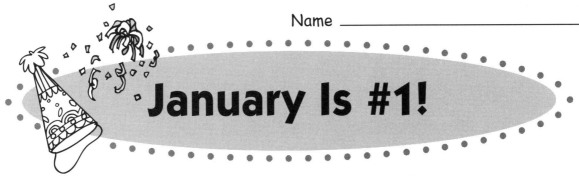

January Is #1!

It's a new year! What year is it? _____

What year will it be in 25 years? _____ How old will you be? _____

Analogies

January is to **month** as **Sunday** is to _____.

January is to **winter** as **July** is to _____.

January is to **February** as **May** is to _____.

This year...

I want to go to _____.

I want to try _____.

I want to learn _____.

I <u>don't</u> want to _____.

I hope _____.

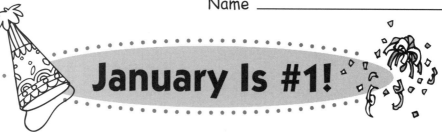

January Is #1!

January is the first month of the year. Can you think of a time when it is good to be first?

_____

When would you <u>not</u> want to be first?

_____

These are Super-Fun New Year's hats.

These are <u>not</u> Super-Fun New Year's hats.

Draw a Super-Fun New Year's hat.

Finish the pattern.

January, March, May, July, _____, _____

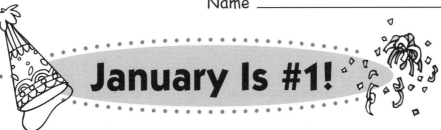

January Is #1!

Louis Braille invented an alphabet of raised dots that blind people feel with their fingers. The Braille Alphabet allows blind people to read.

The Braille Alphabet

a	b	c	d	e	f	g	h	i	j	k	l	m
n	o	p	q	r	s	t	u	v	w	x	y	z

Use the Braille Alphabet to decode a fact about Louis Braille.

_____ _____ _____ _____ _____

_____ _____ _____ _____ .

Write your first name in Braille.

Name _____

February Fun

There are 3 holidays in February. What are they?

1. _____ 2. _____ 3. _____

Which holiday is your favorite? _____

Why? _____

These are Happy Hearts.

These are <u>not</u> Happy Hearts.

Draw a Happy Heart.

Do you like handmade valentines or store-bought valentines?

_____ Why? _____

  Critical and Creative Thinking Activities • EMC 3393 • © Evan-Moor Corp.

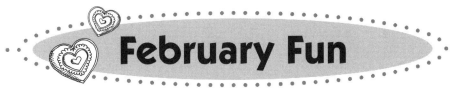

February Fun

Write 4 words to describe the weather right now.

1. _____   3. _____

2. _____   4. _____

How many mistakes can you find on this calendar? Circle them.

February

SUNDAE	MONDAY	WEDNESDAY	TUESDAY	THURSDAY	FRIDAY	SATURDAY
		0	1	2	3	4
5	6	7	ate	9	10	11
12	13 ♡					
14	16	15	17	18		
19	20	21	22	23	24	24
26	27	28	29	30		

How many mistakes did you find? _____

Presidents' Day is in February. If you were the president, what would you do?

_____

_____

February Fun

Kayla made valentines for her friends. Read the clues, and then color each valentine with the correct color.

Christopher

Elisa

Jonathan

River

Amelia

Victoria

Yolanda

Bob

Caroline

Olivia

Robin

Hannah

Eli

Nicholas

Samantha

Forest

Benjamin

Zach

Emma

Bill

Zoe

Rose

- Girls with 8 letters in their names = **blue**

- Boys with 3 syllables in their names = **green**

- Names that could be nouns = **purple**

- Names that begin and end with a vowel = **orange**

- Names that are palindromes (the same backward as forward) = **pink**

- Names that begin with one of the last 3 letters in the alphabet = **red**

Marvelous March

Read the statement about March. Write **A** if it is **always** true. Write **S** if it is **sometimes** true. Write **N** if it is **never** true.

_____ There are 31 days.   _____ It is windy.

_____ It rains.   _____ I wear sandals.

_____ I wear green.   _____ I go trick-or-treating.

The first day of spring is in March. What signs of spring can you see?

_____

_____

_____

_____

_____

_____

Draw a leprechaun. He must be wearing a hat and must be smiling. Write what he is thinking.

Name _____

Marvelous March

It is said that leprechauns bring good luck. What do you think these phrases about luck mean?

"Lucky break" _____

"Lucky charm" _____

"Dumb luck" _____

Complete the 2-word phrases.
Each word <u>must</u> begin with the same letter.
The first word <u>must</u> be an adjective.
The second word <u>must</u> be a noun.
Example: **Marvelous March**

_____ snake

_____ doughnuts

Green _____

Big _____

Add 2 more to the list.

shamrock

broccoli

EXIT sign

leaf

_____

_____

Would you rather be a leprechaun, an elf, or a fairy? _____

Why? _____

Critical and Creative Thinking Activities • EMC 3393 • © Evan-Moor Corp.

Marvelous March

A leprechaun keeps gold in a pot at the end of the rainbow. What other things might be in that pot?

Good things

Bad things

Sticky things

Green things

April Surprises

The lunch ladies played an April Fools' Day joke on the students by scrambling the menu. Unscramble the words to see what is for lunch.

HENKCIC STENUGG _____

LYFFFU CERI _____

ERGEN SNABE _____

LOCOTEACH PIGDUND _____

PALEP CEIJU _____

Look carefully. What do the unscrambled words have in common?

_____

Is it okay to tell a lie on April Fools' Day if it is part of a joke? _____

Why or why not? _____

_____

    Critical and Creative Thinking Activities • EMC 3393 • © Evan-Moor Corp.

April Surprises

nac uoy etirw ruoy eman sdrawkcab?

_____

woh tuoba rouy s'rehcaet eman?

_____

etirw a s'dneirf eman sdrawkcab.

_____

Sydney found 24 eggs in 4 different colors.

- One-third of the eggs were **purple**.

- She found one less **green** egg than the number of **purple** eggs.

- There were twice as many **pink** eggs as **yellow** eggs.

How many did Sydney find of each?

_____ purple eggs

_____ green eggs

_____ pink eggs

_____ yellow eggs

Which egg is different?

April Surprises

On April 1, David could <u>not</u> find any socks to wear! In his empty sock drawer, he found a mysterious note in code. To crack the code, read each letter, and then write the letter that comes just before it in the alphabet. Example: **B** = **A**

Z P V S   T P D L T

___ ___ ___ ___   ___ ___ ___ ___ ___

B S F   J O   U I F

___ ___ ___   ___ ___   ___ ___ ___

G S F F A F S   I B Q Q Z

___ ___ ___ ___ ___ ___ ___ !   ___ ___ ___ ___ ___

B Q S J M   G P P M T   E B Z

___ ___ ___ ___ ___   ___ ___ ___ ___ , ___   ___ ___ ___ !

Critical and Creative Thinking Activities • EMC 3393 • © Evan-Moor Corp.

Hey, It's May!

The answer is **in May**. What is the question?

_____

The answer is **Memorial Day**. What is the question?

_____

Use the clues to find other words that end in **ay**.

24 hours _____ay

buy something _____ay

a cloudy day _____ay

to rot _____ay

not home _____ay

a flowerpot is made of it _____ay

Color the petals. Use 2 colors, and make a pattern. The pattern must be even all the way around the flower. Plan your pattern first.

Hey, It's May!

Write a sentence with exactly 9 words to tell about something you like to do in May.

_____

_____

Of all the months, **May** has the fewest letters. For each number below, write the name of a month that contains that many letters.

③ _May_____

④ _____

⑤ _____

⑥ _____

⑦ _____

⑧ _____

These are Fancy Flowers.

These are <u>not</u> Fancy Flowers.

Draw a Fancy Flower.

 Critical and Creative Thinking Activities • EMC 3393 • © Evan-Moor Corp.

Name _____

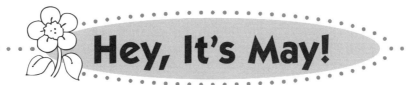

Here is an old saying: "April showers bring May flowers."
To complete the name of each flower below, write the letter from the
rain cloud in the raindrop. You may use each letter only once, so cross
them out as you go. Then unscramble the remaining letters in the cloud
to make the name of another flower. Write it on the line.

A B D E F I L L L N N N O O O R S S U U W Y

R◯S E   V I O◯E T

L I L◯   P◯P P Y

T U◯I P   ◯U T T E R C◯P

D A I◯Y   ◯A N D E L◯O N

P A◯S Y   C A R N◯T I O◯

The name of another flower is _____.

Jazzed About June

What was the most important thing that happened this school year?

_____

_____

How many days of school are left before summer break?

_____

How many hours? _____

When Paris cleaned out her desk at the end of the year, she found 3 quarters, 6 dimes, 5 nickels, and 16 pennies. How much money did Paris find?

$_____

Think about how you did in school this past year. If you improved in it, draw 1 star by it. If you improved <u>a lot</u>, draw 2 stars by it!

math   following directions

writing   computer skills

spelling   keeping things organized

reading   getting along with others

sports   completing work on time

Jazzed About June

Complete the 3 sentences about summer.

I want to _____.

I <u>don't</u> want to _____.

I hope _____.

Analogies

June is to **summer** as **September** is to _____.

June is to **May** as **November** is to _____.

June is to 6 as **January** is to _____.

Next school year, someone else will sit at your desk.
Give 3 pieces of advice to that person about being a student
in this classroom.

1. _____

2. _____

3. _____

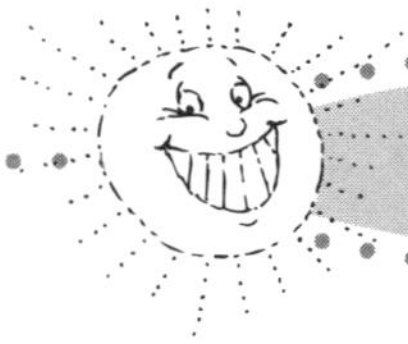

Jazzed About June

Circle one of the choices for each question. Then write why you chose it.

Would you rather cool off in a **pool** or in a **lake**?

_____

_____

Would you rather spend a day in the **woods** or at the **beach**?

_____

_____

Would you rather see a **parade** or a **baseball game**?

_____

_____

Would you rather **go camping with your family** for a week or
go away to a kids' camp for a week?

_____

_____

 Critical and Creative Thinking Activities • EMC 3393 • © Evan-Moor Corp.

Name _____

Monkeys

How would you describe a monkey to someone who has never seen one?

_____

_____

_____

Use the letters in **MONKEYS** to make a word for each clue.

used to unlock _____

dollars and cents _____

opposite of **no** _____

before **two** _____

comes from fire _____

Each monkey at the zoo eats 6 bananas every day. There are 7 monkeys. How many bananas will be needed for...

1 day? _____

2 days? _____

4 days? _____

1 week? _____

Write this sentence correctly.

Matt saw 7 monkies at the zoo.

_____

Monkeys

How are monkeys the same as humans? How are they different?
Fill in the chart with 3 ways for each.

Same	Different

Jane went to Africa to see monkeys. She saw 3 fewer monkeys on the second day than she did on the first day. She saw 6 monkeys on the third day. She saw twice as many monkeys on the first day as she did on the third day. How many monkeys did Jane see on each day? How many monkeys in all?

First day: _____

Second day: _____

Third day: _____

In all: _____

What is this?

_____

_____

Monkeys

Monkey begins with **MON**. Each of the answers to the clues also contain **MON**. Use the clues to complete the words. Then write the letters with numbers under them at the bottom of this page to find the kind of monkey that you see there.

expensive gem   ____ ____ ____ M O N ____
                                       3

popular board game   M O N ____ ____ ____ ____ ____
                                      2   8   12

12 in a year   M O N ____ ____ ____
                                       1

rare or unusual   ____ ____ ____ ____ ____ M O N
                                 9   7

scary creature   M O N ____ ____ ____ ____
                                          6

type of nut   ____ ____ M O N ____
                                        4

yellow fruit   ____ ____ ____ M O N
                                  11

coins and bills   M O N ____ ____
                                    5

Japanese robe   ____ ____ M O N ____
                             10

____ ____ ____ ____ ____ ____   ____ ____ ____ ____ ____ ____
1   2   3   4   5   6   7   8   9   10   11   12

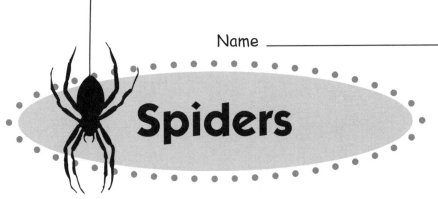

Name _____

Spiders

Why do you think so many people are afraid of spiders?

_____

What are 3 problems that you might have if you had 8 legs like a spider?

1. _____

2. _____

3. _____

Which spider is missing a leg? Circle it.

Analogies

Spider is to **web** as bear is to _____.

Spider is to **fly** as cat is to _____.

Spider is to **eight** as cow is to _____.

Critical and Creative Thinking Activities • EMC 3393 • © Evan-Moor Corp.

Spiders

Fill in the blank to solve each 8 problem.

1 ____ + 6 − 2 = 8

2 3 + 12 − ____ = 8

3 20 − ____ − 5 = 8

4 9 − ____ + 3 = 8

5 6 + ____ − ____ = 8

6 14 − ____ − ____ = 8

7 ____ + ____ − ____ = 8

8 ____ − ____ − ____ = 8

Draw a spider web in the top right corner.

Draw a spider hanging from the web.

What is the spider looking for?

_____

Write a sentence about spiders. Use exactly 5 words.

_____

Write a sentence using the words **spider**, **fly**, and **black**.

_____

Spiders

This spider has caught a lot of flies in her web! Show how the spider can get to each of the 8 flies and then back to the center of her web without crossing her own path.

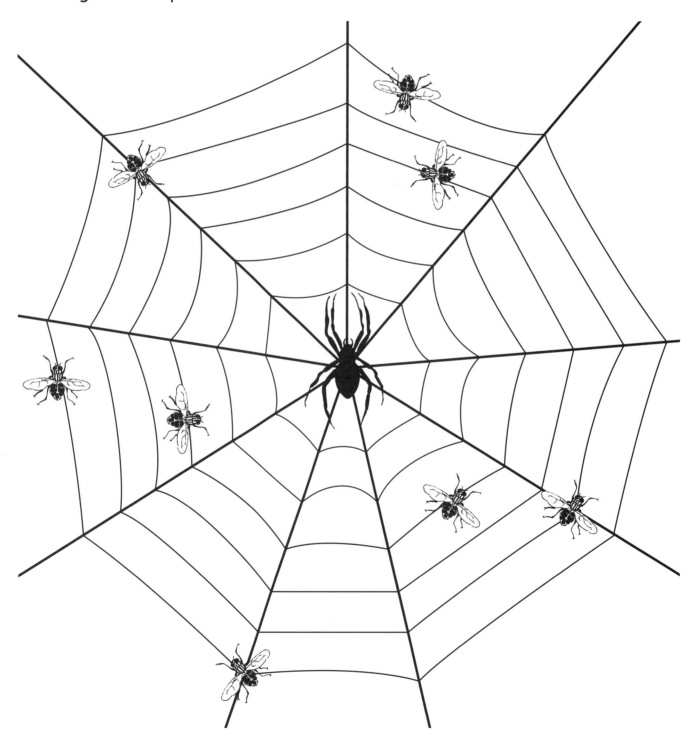

Critical and Creative Thinking Activities • EMC 3393 • © Evan-Moor Corp.

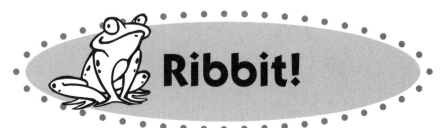

Ribbit!

Show how a tadpole becomes a frog.

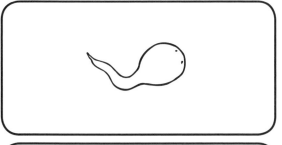

What does it mean to "have a frog in your throat"?

_____

_____

How many flies did Fred Frog catch? Here are some clues:

- He caught more than a dozen.
- He caught an odd number.
- He caught fewer than 17.
- The number he caught was <u>not</u> three more than 10.

Fred caught _____ flies.

Write 1 true sentence and 1 false sentence about frogs.

_____

_____

_____

_____

Name _____

Ribbit!

Oh dear, your big sister kissed a frog and he turned into a prince! But, while he was a frog, someone took over his kingdom. So now he is hanging out at your house all day, watching TV and eating everything. What can you do?

_____

_____

Read the clue. Write the word that rhymes with **frog**.

pig _____

poodle _____

dead tree _____

slow run _____

wooden shoe _____

What is wrong with this sentence?

> The baby frogs hopped away as soon as they hatched.

_____

_____

_____

Analogies

Hop is to **frog** as _____ is to **bird**.

Green is to **frog** as _____ is to **elephant**.

Swamp is to **frog** as _____ is to **whale**.

   Critical and Creative Thinking Activities • EMC 3393 • © Evan-Moor Corp.

Ribbit!

Fannie Frog is really smart! She hops <u>only</u> on the lily pads with correct answers. Color her path across the pond.

Start

$4 \times 6 = 36$

$2 \times 6 = 22$

$7 \times 6 = 42$

$8 \times 4 = 32$

$5 \times 9 = 45$

$5 \times 6 = 30$

$4 \times 2 = 12$

$4 \times 4 = 18$

$7 \times 7 = 49$

$6 \times 4 = 24$

$7 \times 2 = 14$

$8 \times 2 = 14$

$9 \times 4 = 36$

$7 \times 7 = 47$

$7 \times 6 = 56$

$7 \times 5 = 35$

$3 \times 9 = 27$

$6 \times 6 = 36$

$5 \times 9 = 35$

$9 \times 4 = 46$

$3 \times 6 = 18$

$7 \times 8 = 58$

$7 \times 9 = 53$

$7 \times 6 = 48$

$2 \times 7 = 16$

$4 \times 5 = 20$

$3 \times 6 = 21$

$2 \times 6 = 10$

$5 \times 4 = 30$

$5 \times 6 = 30$

$8 \times 8 = 64$

$2 \times 9 = 18$

$5 \times 6 = 35$

$4 \times 4 = 18$

$3 \times 9 = 28$

$7 \times 8 = 56$

$9 \times 6 = 53$

$4 \times 7 = 26$

$9 \times 8 = 62$

$8 \times 8 = 66$

$5 \times 5 = 25$

$8 \times 6 = 48$

$7 \times 9 = 63$

$9 \times 6 = 54$

$3 \times 8 = 24$

$5 \times 8 = 45$

$9 \times 9 = 81$

$7 \times 1 = 8$

$7 \times 3 = 31$

Finish

© Evan-Moor Corp. • EMC 3393 • Critical and Creative Thinking Activities

Pets

How many different kinds of pets can you name? Use the back if you need to.

1. _____   4. _____   7. _____

2. _____   5. _____   8. _____

3. _____   6. _____   9. _____

Circle the kinds of pets you own. Draw a star next to the other kinds of pets you'd like to own.

• •

Write what these fish are thinking.

Write 5 other words like **pet** that begin with **p** and end in **t**.

P_____t

P_____t

P_____t

P_____t

P_____t

     Critical and Creative Thinking Activities • EMC 3393 • © Evan-Moor Corp.

Pets

Would you rather own a dog or a cat? _____

Why? _____

What kind of pet are they?

iguana, snake, turtle _____

canary, parrot, dove _____

rat, gerbil, hamster _____

beagle, lab, hound _____

Raul has 2 kinds of pets: dogs and birds. One day, Raul counted his pets' heads and legs. There were 9 heads and 22 legs. How many dogs and birds does Raul have?

_____ dogs

_____ birds

Write 1 good thing and 1 bad thing about owning each kind of pet.

Pet	Good thing	Bad thing
Fish		
Hamster		
Parakeet		
Dog		

© Evan-Moor Corp. • EMC 3393 • Critical and Creative Thinking Activities

Pets

Each of these 6 children has a different pet. Read the clues.
Then write the child's name under his or her pet.
Hint: You will need to read the clues at least 2 times.

| Charlie | Claire | Jack | Kate | Sawyer | Shannon |

- **Kate** is allergic to dogs.

- **Jack's** pet does not have legs.

- **Shannon's** pet lives in a cage.

- **Kate's** pet has 4 legs.

- **Charlie** and **Sawyer** each have a kind of pet that begins with the same letter as their names.

_____

_____   _____   _____

Critical and Creative Thinking Activities • EMC 3393 • © Evan-Moor Corp.

Reptiles

Number the reptiles from 1 to 7 according to how dangerous you think they are. The <u>most</u> dangerous one should be number 1.

_____ crocodile

_____ iguana

_____ rattlesnake

_____ snapping turtle

_____ gecko

_____ boa constrictor

_____ sea turtle

What reptile did Jim see at the zoo? Read the clues and cross out letters. Then use the leftover letters to write the name of the reptile.

- Cross out the last 2 letters of the alphabet.

- Cross out every letter that is made with exactly 2 straight lines.

- Cross out the letters in Jim's name.

Jim saw a _____.

Would you rather be a crocodile, a boa constrictor, or a sea turtle?

Which one? _____

Why? _____

Reptiles

The answer is **a chameleon**. What is the question?

_____

The answer is **a pile of snakes**. What is the question?

_____

The answer is **a pair of sea turtles**. What is the question?

_____

Use the letters in **ALLIGATOR** to make a word for each clue.

not short _____

You're it! _____

decompose _____

sick _____

hiking path _____

Draw another snake so that the pair of them is symmetrical (if you folded on the dotted line, the snakes would match up.). Then name the snakes.

_____   _____

 Critical and Creative Thinking Activities • EMC 3393 • © Evan-Moor Corp.

Reptiles

Turn a **lizard** into a **turtle** in just 6 steps. Read each clue and rewrite the word. Change only one letter on each line until you have a **turtle**!

	L	I	Z	A	R	D
Change the 4th letter in the alphabet to the 5th.						
Change the 3rd letter to an **R**.						
Change the letter with just 2 straight lines to a **T**.						
Make the 4th letter the same as the 1st letter.						
Make the 5th letter into an **L**.						
Make **I** into the last vowel in the alphabet.						

Quack!

How is a duck the same as:

a swan? _____

a sea turtle? _____

a bat? _____

How many ducklings does each mama duck have? **Drew** has more ducklings than **Dora**. **Drew** has fewer ducklings than **Denise**.

_____ has 6 ducklings.

_____ has 7 ducklings.

_____ has 8 ducklings.

How many ducklings do the 3 mama ducks have altogether?

_____ ducklings

There are twice as many *girl* ducklings as boy ducklings.

_____ girl ducklings

_____ boy ducklings

Unscramble the words to make a sentence.

fly   winter   for   ducks   south   the

_____

_____

    Critical and Creative Thinking Activities • EMC 3393 • © Evan-Moor Corp.

Name _____

Quack!

Complete the 3 sentences.

Those ducks _____.

_____ a duck _____.

_____ the ducklings.

Help the ducklings find their mother. Trace each duckling's path with a different color.

What are 2 other birds that can both swim __and__ fly?

1. _____   2. _____

© Evan-Moor Corp. • EMC 3393 • Critical and Creative Thinking Activities

Mama Duck has lost her ducklings. Follow the directions below to help her find them. When you find each duckling, write the number in the square. Start from the center of the grid each time.

 1 2 North then 4 West

 2 3 East then 3 South

 3 1 South then 4 West

 4 3 North then 5 East

 5 2 East then 3 South then 4 West

 6 3 North then 2 West then 5 South

 7 5 East then 2 North then 3 West

 8 3 South then 4 East then 4 North

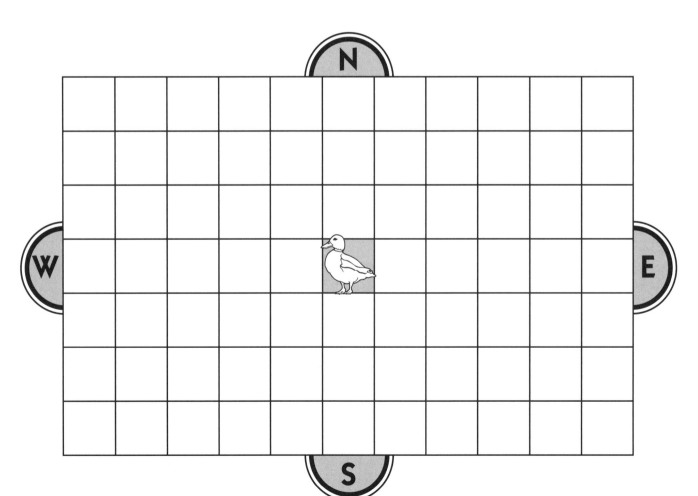

Critical and Creative Thinking Activities • EMC 3393 • © Evan-Moor Corp.

Slugs and Worms

How are slugs and worms the same? How are they different?
Write 3 ways for each.

Same	Different

Finish these tongue twisters. Use as many words as you can.

Sally Slug saw _____.

Willy Worm went _____.

Josie lined up 5 worms end to end.
Then she lined up 7 slugs the same
way. Each worm is 5 inches long, and
each slug is 4 inches long. Which line
is longer? Circle.

worms   slugs

How much longer? _____ inches

If you had to eat either 3 worms
or 1 slug, which would you
choose?

_____

Why? _____

_____

Name _____

Slugs and Worms

Use the letters in the words **slugs** and **worms** to make more words. Each new word <u>must</u> use letters from both words and <u>must</u> be 4 or more letters long.

SLUGS

_____

_____

_____

_____

WORMS

_____

_____

_____

_____

Aaron is gathering worms for his family's compost bin. He found 14 worms on Monday and twice as many on Tuesday. On Wednesday, he found half as many as he did on Monday and Tuesday together. How many worms did Aaron find?

Monday: _____

Tuesday: _____

Wednesday: _____

All 3 days: _____

Draw worms to form the letters in the word **worm**. Then draw slugs to make the word **slug**.

Critical and Creative Thinking Activities • EMC 3393 • © Evan-Moor Corp.

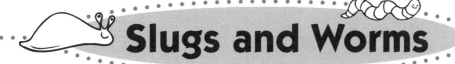

Slugs and Worms

Use the slugs and the worms in the box to make words. Then write the words on the lines. You may use the same slugs and worms more than once.

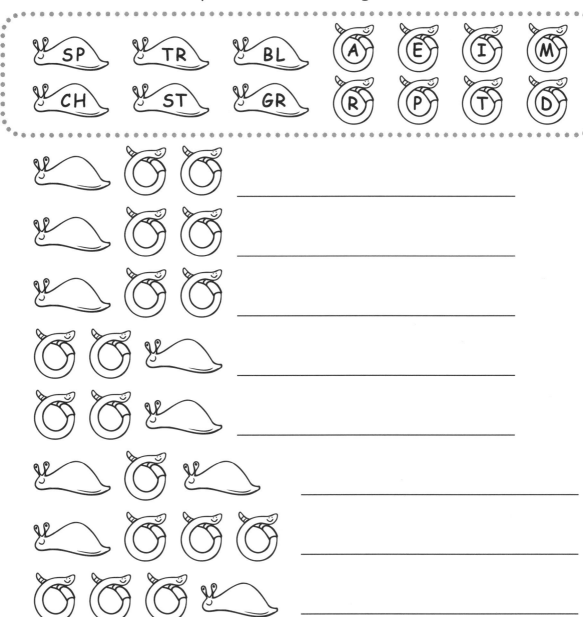

Make up one of your own.

_____

Name _____

Bzzzzzzz

A bee is buzzing near you and it won't go away. What should you do? Rate these ideas from 1 to 6. The best idea should be number 1.

_____ Run away.

_____ Stand as still as possible.

_____ Scream.

_____ Ignore it.

_____ Sing it a song.

_____ Swat it.

Complete the words that begin with **be**.

Look out be_____!

Be_____ of the dog.

Be_____ in yourself.

He was be_____ himself.

To infinity and be_____!

Just be_____ you and me...

Be_____ I said so!

Look be_____ you leap.

Write 3 kinds of sentences about bees.

Boring: _____

Interesting: _____

Silly: _____

   Critical and Creative Thinking Activities • EMC 3393 • © Evan-Moor Corp.

Name _____

Bzzzzzzz

Analogies

Bee is to sting as mosquito is to _____.

Bee is to hive as bird is to _____.

Bee is to yellow as polar bear is to _____.

Bees can sting. What are 3 other animals that can sting?

1. _____   2. _____   3. _____

Bees have stripes. What are 3 other animals that have stripes?

1. _____   2. _____   3. _____

Betty Bee is an odd bee. She will gather nectar only from the flowers with odd-numbered products. Color the correct flowers.

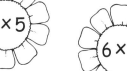

4×5 6×4 7×5 6×8 3×8

7×3 9×7 2×7 7×7 9×3

© Evan-Moor Corp. • EMC 3393 • Critical and Creative Thinking Activities

Bzzzzzzzz

Bonnie Bee is gathering letters instead of nectar! Read the clues to find the letters she gathered. Write the letters in order on the lines below to solve the riddle.

- top right corner

- just to the right of **Z**

- two flowers down from **G**

- just above **A**

- down and to the left of **T**

- bottom center

- up and to the left of **X**

- down and to the left of **L**

- down and to the left of **Q**

What kind of gum does a bee chew?

___ ___ ___ ___ ___ ___ ___ ___ ___!

   Critical and Creative Thinking Activities • EMC 3393 • © Evan-Moor Corp.

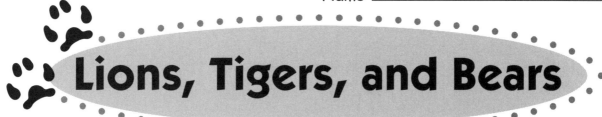

Lions, Tigers, and Bears

Write 3 words to describe each animal. Try <u>not</u> to use the same word more than once.

Lion _____   _____   _____

Tiger _____   _____   _____

Bear _____   _____   _____

Eli is at the zoo. He sees the bears before he eats lunch. He sees the lions before the bears. He sees the tigers after lunch. Write what Eli does in the correct order.

First: _____

Second: _____

Third: _____

Fourth: _____

Cross out the letters from the words **lions**, **tigers**, and **bears**. Be sure to cross out each letter only once. Then unscramble the leftover letters to find out what these 3 kinds of animals have in common.

N S I R S T B O B E S C L S E U I R G A

Lions, tigers, and bears all have _____.

Lions, Tigers, and Bears

Would you rather be a lion, a tiger, or a bear? _____

Why? _____

_____

What would a lion-tiger-bear look like? Draw it.

How many fish did Boris Bear eat?

- He ate fewer than 21 fish.

- The number of fish he ate was <u>not</u> odd.

- He ate more than 14 fish.

- The number of fish he ate <u>cannot</u> be divided evenly by 4.

Boris ate _____ fish.

Lions, tigers, and bears are sometimes in books, movies, and on TV. Winnie the Pooh is one example. How many more can you name?

1. _____   4. _____

2. _____   5. _____

3. _____   6. _____

     Critical and Creative Thinking Activities • EMC 3393 • © Evan-Moor Corp.

Name _____

Lions, Tigers, and Bears

Read each numbered item. Write the number where it belongs in the Venn diagram. Make up one of your own for number 14. Then write 14 where it belongs in the diagram.

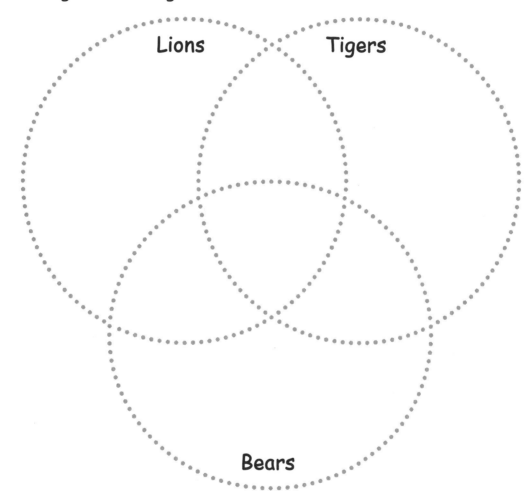

1. has stripes
2. likes water
3. hibernates
4. eats meat
5. roars

6. eats berries
7. has a mane
8. has sharp teeth
9. can climb trees
10. lives in a cave

11. can be dark brown
12. can have black fur
13. has a long tail
14. _____

© Evan-Moor Corp. • EMC 3393 • Critical and Creative Thinking Activities

Name _____

Ocean Life

Fish are animals that have backbones and that breathe underwater using gills instead of lungs. How many animals can you name that live in the ocean that are <u>not</u> fish? Use the back if you need more space.

1. _____

2. _____

3. _____

4. _____

5. _____

6. _____

What does this say?

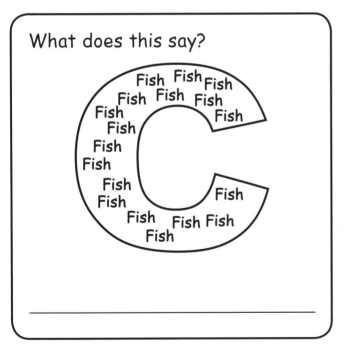

_____

Fish ends in **sh**. Use the clues to find these other words that end in **sh**.

plate   _____sh

quiet   _____sh

car accident _____sh

in a hurry   _____sh

garbage   _____sh

for hair   _____sh

for a dog   _____sh

Sheldon Shark ate 74 little fish. 27 were green and 19 were orange. How many fish did he eat that were <u>not</u> green or orange?

_____ fish

     Critical and Creative Thinking Activities • EMC 3393 • © Evan-Moor Corp.

Ocean Life

Complete the 3 sentences.

The playful dolphins _____.

_____ 4 small fish _____.

_____ a hermit crab.

Name something that lives
in the ocean that...

is big _____

is gray _____

is orange _____

is fast _____

has claws _____

is dangerous _____

Number the sea creatures
from 1 to 5 by size. The
smallest one should be
number 1.

_____ dolphin

_____ whale

_____ hermit crab

_____ octopus

_____ lobster

Finish the tongue twisters.

Six seals saw _____.

Willy Whale went _____.

Ocean Life

Read the clues to find the correct fish.
Write the letters in order on the lines
below to solve the riddle.

- fish with the biggest spotted tail

- skinny fish with black fins

- skinny fish with a big tail

- fish with spots and teeth

- fat fish with big fins and no spots

- sad fish with a spotted tail

- sad, skinny fish with dark fins

- striped fish with teeth

- fat fish with teeth and no fins

- striped fish with a big tail

- fish with stripes and a small tail

Why is a fish easy to weigh?

___ ___ ___ ___ ___ ___ ___ ___ ___ ___ ___ ___ ___ ___ ___ ___!

Critical and Creative Thinking Activities • EMC 3393 • © Evan-Moor Corp.

Home Sweet Home

Analogies

Picture is to **wall** as **rug** is to _____.

Toilet is to **bathroom** as **oven** is to _____.

House is to **family** as **school** is to _____.

What is your favorite room in your house? _____

Why? _____

What color is each of these things in your house?

front door _____

refrigerator _____

couch _____

bathroom counter _____

How many of each of these things are in your house?

closets _____

chairs _____

drawers _____

windows _____

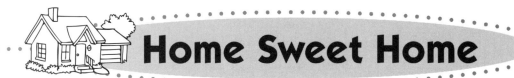

Home Sweet Home

Cody's family has moved twice, and he has lived in 3 different houses. The **green** house was <u>not</u> on Maple Street. The **blue** house was <u>not</u> on Spruce Street. The **red** house was <u>not</u> on Maple Street or Spruce Street.

What colors were Cody's houses?

Maple Street: _____

Spruce Street: _____

Elm Street: _____

If you could change one thing about your house, what would it be?

_____

Why? _____

What does this say?

Home Home

Range

_____

If there were a fire or a flood at your house and you knew that all of the people and animals were safe, what 3 things would you save?

1. _____

2. _____

3. _____

Home Sweet Home

Color the grid to find the hidden picture.

	1	2	3	4	5	6	7	8	9
A									
B									
C									
D									
E									
F									
G									
H									
I									
J									

A5 = red

J2–J5 = blue

H7–J7 = green

D2–D8 = red

G3 = yellow

F2–I2 = blue

A7–B7 = brown

I3–I5 = blue

E1–E9 = red

H4 = yellow

F5–H5 = blue

G6–G8 = blue

B4–B6 = red

H8–J8 = blue

F3–F4 = blue

H3 = yellow

C3–C7 = red

F6–F8 = blue

H6–J6 = green

G4 = yellow

© Evan-Moor Corp. • EMC 3393 • Critical and Creative Thinking Activities

In Our Classroom

Put the classroom things in order according to how close they are to your desk right now. The item that is closest should be number 1. The item that is farthest should be number 6.

_____ the main door   _____ a window

_____ whiteboard/chalkboard   _____ your math book

_____ hooks for coats   _____ the pencil sharpener

Think about your classroom and your bedroom. How are they the same? How are they different? Fill in the chart.

Same	Different

If you could change one thing about your classroom, what would it be?

_____

Why? _____

Critical and Creative Thinking Activities • EMC 3393 • © Evan-Moor Corp.

Name _____

In Our Classroom

Name something in your classroom that is:

round _____

sharp _____

soft _____

colorful _____

tiny _____

loud _____

The purpose of a classroom is to provide a place for learning. What are the 5 most important things in your classroom that help you learn?

1. _____

2. _____

3. _____

4. _____

5. _____

If your desk could talk, what would it say? Write it.

Add as many words as you can.

pencil, crayon, chalk, _____

teacher, janitor, nurse, _____

math, spelling, science, _____

In Our Classroom

Look around your classroom for things that are made from wood, metal, and plastic. Write the names of at least 12 things in the Venn diagram. Try to fill each section with the name of at least one thing.

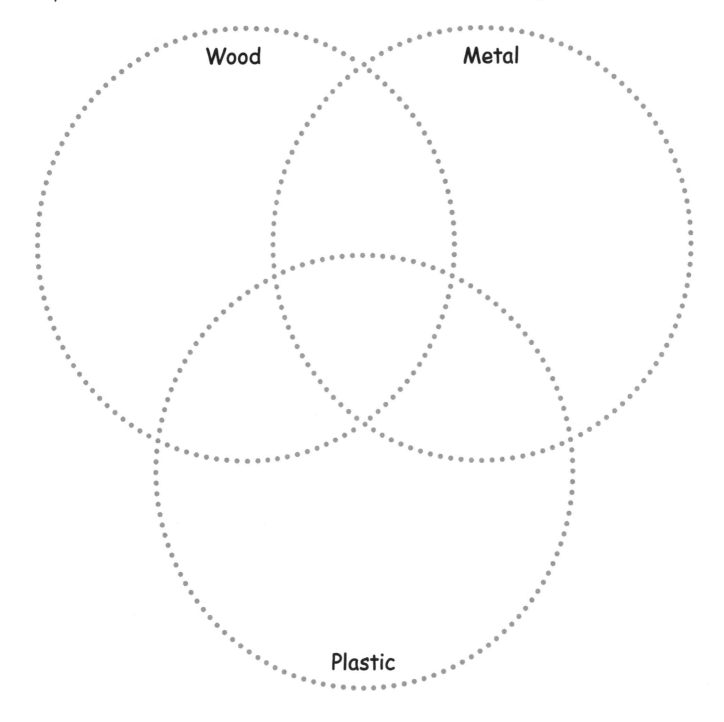

Critical and Creative Thinking Activities • EMC 3393 • © Evan-Moor Corp.

In the Woods

Shh… What can you hear in the woods? Write 3 things.

1. _____   2. _____   3. _____

Write a sentence about the woods. Use exactly 7 words.

_____

Forest is another word for **woods**. What are other words for these things you might find in the woods?

rabbit _____

trail _____

creek _____

stone _____

twig _____

burrow _____

You are going for a hike in the woods. Circle the 3 most important things to bring.

compass   book   binoculars

whistle   map   first-aid kit

water   hat   flashlight

bug spray   snack

If you walk 3 miles in an hour, how far will you walk in 90 minutes?

_____ miles

Name _____

In the Woods

Add 2 more to each list.

raccoon, deer, rabbit, _____, _____

beetle, mosquito, butterfly, _____, _____

Name something in the woods that is....

soft _____

hard _____

rough _____

sharp _____

What does this say?

A
WO walk **ODS**

_____

_____

Draw lines to match the animals with their descriptions.
Be careful: You may match only one description to each animal.

woodpecker   nocturnal

squirrel   bushy tail

deer   long ears

raccoon   black and white

rabbit   can fly

owl   eats bugs

skunk   climbs trees

tree frog   brown

In the Woods

Use the names of trees to fill in the puzzle. Plan carefully.

	P				
	I				
	N				
	E				

3 letters

ASH
ELM
FIR
OAK

4 letters

PALM
~~PINE~~

5 letters

BEECH
BIRCH
CEDAR
MAPLE
PEACH

6 letters

CHERRY
ORANGE
SPRUCE
WALNUT
WILLOW

7 letters

DOGWOOD
HEMLOCK
HICKORY
REDWOOD

At a Party

The answer is **a big party**. What is the question?

_____

Write a sentence using the words **party**, **cake**, and **sister**.

_____

_____

Number these things you might do at a party from 1 to 6. The one you like the most should be number 1.

_____ see friends

_____ play games

_____ wear special clothes

_____ meet new people

_____ eat yummy food

_____ see presents opened

Nikki had a lot of balloons at her party.

• There were 3 times as many **red** balloons as **blue** balloons.

• There were 6 more **green** balloons than **blue** balloons.

• There were 14 **green** balloons.

How many balloons of each color were there?

_____ red balloons

_____ blue balloons

_____ green balloons

At a Party

James is going to a party, but there is something wrong with the directions. Help him find the party by rewriting the directions with the spaces in the correct places.

Dir ecti onst oth ep arty: _____

Dri venor thdo wnMa inStreet.   _____

Tur nlef tonEl mAve nue.   _____

Dri vef iveb locks.   _____

Loo kfo rth ere dho us e.   _____

Yo ua reh ere! Co meo nin!   _____

Analogies

Eat is to **cake** as _____ is to **soda**.

Hit is to **piñata** as _____ is to **donkey**.

Hokeypokey is to **dance** as _____ is to **game**.

P is for **party**.
How many **p**'s were on this page before you started to write? _____

At a Party

You are throwing a party! Design a cover for the invitation. Then plan what you will need for the party and what your guests will do at the party.

Invitation

Make a list of what you will need for your party.

_____

_____

_____

_____

_____

_____

_____

_____

_____

_____

_____

_____

What will your guests do at the party?

_____

_____

_____

_____

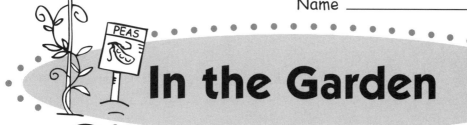

In the Garden

You can plant 4 things in your garden. What will you plant?

1. _____   3. _____

2. _____   4. _____

Jason planted 12 tomato plants. There were about 15 tomatoes on each of Jason's plants. About how many tomatoes did Jason harvest?

 about _____ tomatoes

What are 3 things that Jason can make with his tomatoes?

1. _____

2. _____

3. _____

Can you think of a vegetable for each of these letters?

S _____

A _____

P _____

C _____

L _____

B _____

R _____

Z _____

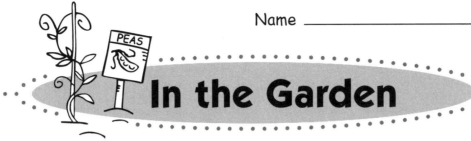

In the Garden

Grant planted his favorite kind of vegetable. Cross out the letters of the vegetables that he did <u>not</u> plant to find the one that he <u>did</u> plant.

E N Y S N Q R O L U E O A C I R O S C N H

He did <u>not</u> plant **CELERY**.

He did <u>not</u> plant **ONION**.

He did <u>not</u> plant **CORN**.

Grant planted

_____.

Oh no! Bunnies are eating your vegetables. What can you do?

_____

What vegetables are these?

 + N _____

○ + 🪴 _____

 + A + 👣 _____

In his garden, Alvin picked 27 zucchinis, 14 carrots, 22 apples, 18 onions, and 43 potatoes. How many vegetables did Alvin harvest?

_____ vegetables

Critical and Creative Thinking Activities • EMC 3393 • © Evan-Moor Corp.

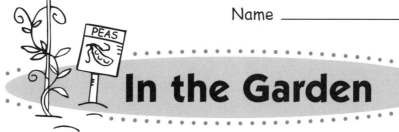

In the Garden

Help Zoe plan her garden. Use the clues to find where each type of seed should be planted. Then write the vegetable names where they belong in the garden.

- Peas and beans should be planted in long rows.

- Zucchini should be planted west of the pumpkins.

- Tomatoes should be planted farthest to the east to get the morning sun.

- Peas are planted early, so they should be planted along the edge of the garden.

- Carrots should be planted south of the beans.

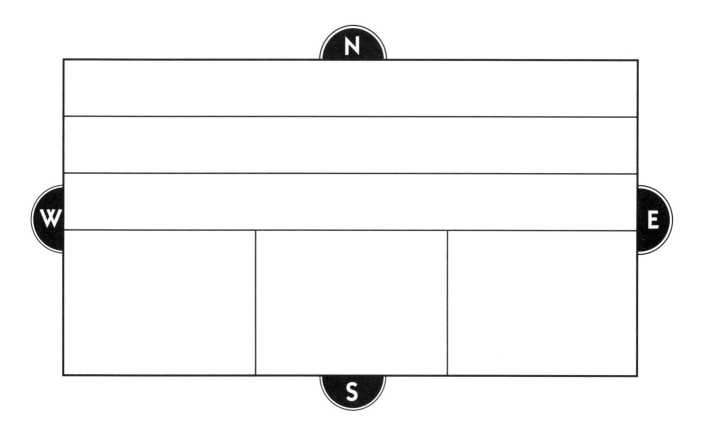

Pizza Time

How many equal slices can be cut from each pizza?

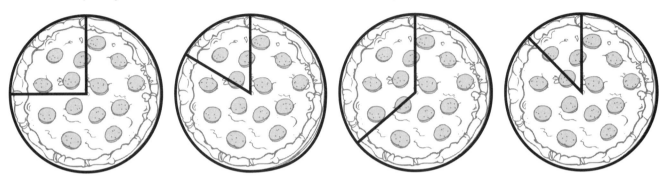

_____   _____   _____   _____

Help Lucy make sure that she has enough pizza for her party. She invited 15 people. She ordered 3 pizzas. Each pizza has 12 slices. Each person (including Lucy) gets 2 slices.

Number of slices needed: _____

Number of slices in all 3 pizzas: _____   Enough pizza? _____

Besides being food, what does a pizza have in common with...

a hamburger? _____

spaghetti and meat sauce? _____

a cookie? _____

   Critical and Creative Thinking Activities • EMC 3393 • © Evan-Moor Corp.

Pizza Time

Write a sentence that is always true about pizza.

_____

Write a sentence that is sometimes true about pizza.

_____

Write a sentence that is <u>never</u> true about pizza.

_____

A pizza is flat and round. Can you think of 5 other things that are also flat and round?

1. _____

2. _____

3. _____

4. _____

5. _____

Someone went crazy with the pizza slicer. How many shapes with 3 sides can you find?

Hint: There may be smaller pieces inside of larger pieces.

_____

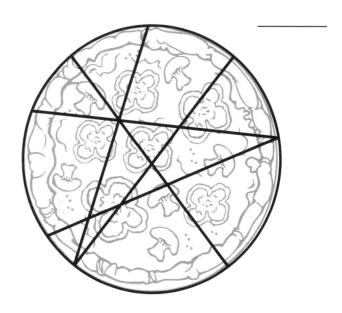

Pizza Time

Dave had 5 pizzas to deliver. Read the clues. Then number the pizzas in the order they were delivered.

- Dave delivered a meat pizza first.

- He delivered a pizza with mushrooms last.

- He delivered the Canadian bacon pizza after delivering the cheese pizza.

- He delivered the pizza with mushrooms and green peppers after delivering the pepperoni pizza.

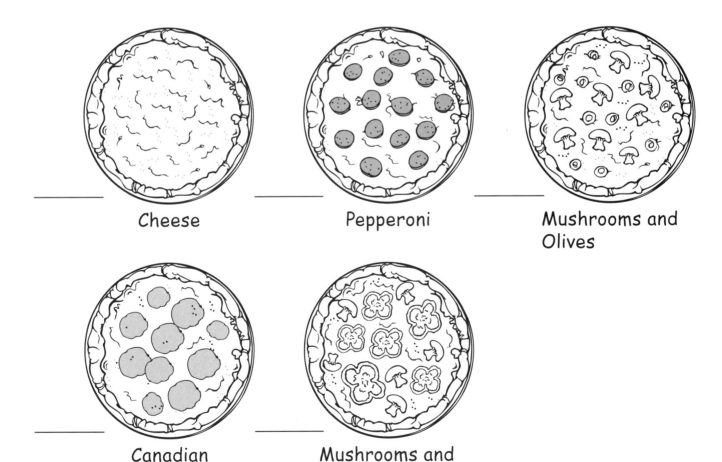

Cheese

Pepperoni

Mushrooms and Olives

Canadian Bacon

Mushrooms and Green Peppers

Critical and Creative Thinking Activities • EMC 3393 • © Evan-Moor Corp.

Name _____

Lunchtime

Which is better, school hot lunch or lunch from home? _____

Why? _____

Invent the worst sandwich of all time. What will you put in it?

_____

_____

_____

_____

_____

Julie, Janie, and Jenny each had a different fruit in their lunches. Draw lines to match each girl with the correct fruit.

- Jenny's fruit was <u>not</u> red.
- Janie's fruit was <u>not</u> round.

Julie   banana

Janie   orange

Jenny   apple

Write a sentence using the words **sandwich**, **apple**, **milk**, and **elephant**.

_____

_____

Lunchtime

Design the perfect lunch! Draw each item on the plate, and then label what you drew.

Is your perfect lunch healthy?

_____

Why or why not? _____

_____

_____

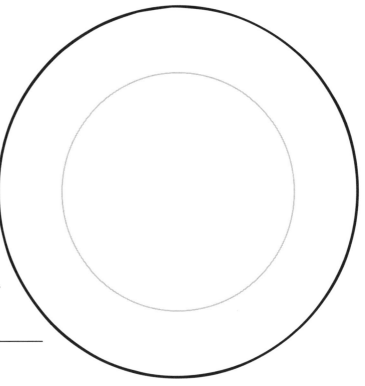

Analogies

Straw is to milk as spoon is to _____.

Milk is to cow as juice is to _____.

Noon is to lunch as evening is to _____.

Continue the food chain. Each new word **must** begin with the letter that the last word ended in.

banana → apricot → turkey → yam → _____ → _____

→ _____ → _____ → _____ → _____

  Critical and Creative Thinking Activities • EMC 3393 • © Evan-Moor Corp.

Lunchtime

How many different lunch combinations can you make? Each lunch **must** include a sandwich, a piece of fruit, and a drink.

Sandwiches	Fruit	Drinks
PB & J	Apple	Milk
Tuna	Banana	Juice

1. _____ _____ _____

2. _____ _____ _____

3. _____ _____ _____

4. _____ _____ _____

5. _____ _____ _____

6. _____ _____ _____

7. _____ _____ _____

8. _____ _____ _____

Challenge: What if you added an orange to the list of fruit choices? Write the new combinations on the back.

Eat Your Veggies

There are many kinds of vegetables! Circle the ones you like. Cross off the ones you do <u>not</u> like. Underline the ones you have never tried.

carrots	zucchini	spinach
lettuce	peas	beets
broccoli	asparagus	celery
cucumber	cauliflower	green beans

Draw a star next to the vegetable that you like best.

You are making vegetable soup. What vegetables will you use?

_____

_____

_____

_____

_____

_____

Rachel ate exactly 23 peas from 6 pods. Circle the 6 pods.

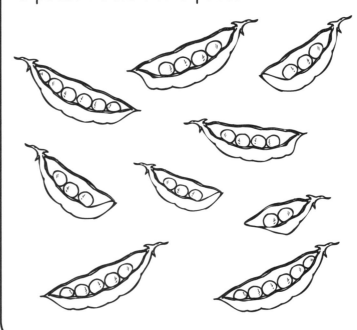

 Critical and Creative Thinking Activities • EMC 3393 • © Evan-Moor Corp.

Eat Your Veggies

Write a sentence that is true about vegetables.

_____

Write a sentence that is <u>not</u> true about vegetables.

_____

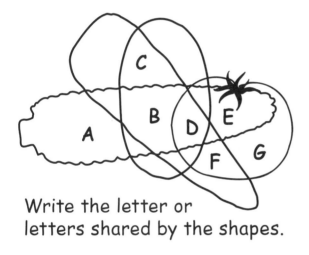

Write the letter or
letters shared by the shapes.

carrot and potato _____

corn and tomato _____

potato, corn,
and carrot _____

all 4 vegetables _____

1 vegetable each _____

Use the clues about vegetables to
fill in the missing letters.

grows underground

C ____ ____ ____ ____ T

grows in heads

L ____ ____ ____ ____ ____ E

long and skinny

B ____ ____ ____ S

used to make pickles

C ____ ____ ____ ____ ____ ____ ____ R

© Evan-Moor Corp. • EMC 3393 • Critical and Creative Thinking Activities

Eat Your Veggies

Read the clues and cross off the words. Then write the leftover words in order from left to right to answer the riddle at the bottom of this page.

- Cross off the words that begin with **M**.

- Cross off the names of fruits.

- Cross off the words that end in **ing**.

- Cross off the adverbs.

- Cross off the words that rhyme with **beet**.

PEACH	THE	SWEET	CABBAGE	TAKING
SADLY	MOUSE	WOULD	EAT	WIN
THE	BANANA	MUST	RACE	TREAT
RUNNING	STREET	BECAUSE	MAKE	APPLE
NEAT	IT	FEET	QUICKLY	IS
MILE	QUIETLY	WINNING	AHEAD	MANGO

If a carrot and a cabbage were in a race, which one would win?

_____

_____

Critical and Creative Thinking Activities • EMC 3393 • © Evan-Moor Corp.

Name _____

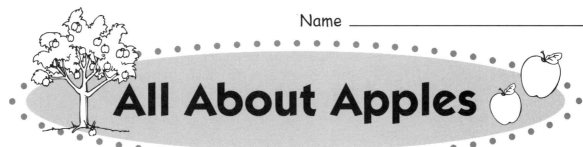
All About Apples

List 6 adjectives to describe an apple.

1. _____   4. _____

2. _____   5. _____

3. _____   6. _____

Which state produces the most apples? To find out, circle the different types of apples in this mini word search. Then unscramble the remaining letters to make the name of a state.

```
J  O  N  A  G  O  L  D  G  R
W  N  A  H  A  O  T  S  N  O
P  I  N  K  L  A  D  Y  I  M
J  O  N  A  T  H  A  N  E
```

Rome   Jonagold   Pink Lady   Gala   Jonathan

The state that produces the most apples is _____.

The word **apple** has double **p**'s. What are the names of 3 other foods with double letters?

1. _____   2. _____   3. _____

© Evan-Moor Corp. • EMC 3393 • *Critical and Creative Thinking Activities*   89

All About Apples

Write a sentence that is always true about apples.

_____

Write a sentence that is sometimes true about apples.

_____

Write a sentence that is <u>never</u> true about apples.

_____

Jonah has 37 apples. He wants to use them to make apple pies. It takes 8 apples to make a pie. How many pies can Jonah make?

_____ pies

How many apples will be left over?

_____ leftover apples

Draw an apple. Then write what the apple would say if it could talk.

How many times is the word **apples** written on this page? _____

Name _____

Add **+** and **−** signs to make each equation true.

9   6 = 3   4   3 = 7

6   8   5 = 9   16   8   2 = 10

8   3   7 = 12   5   3   7 = 9

4   9   6 = 7   6   6   3 = 15

15   6   4 = 5   17   9   4 = 4

3   7   6   1 = 3

4   5   9   2   3 = 5

9   4   3   4   7   3 = 8

© Evan-Moor Corp. • EMC 3393 • Critical and Creative Thinking Activities

Name _____

I Scream for Ice Cream

Invent an ice-cream flavor. Name it. _____

What is in it? _____

Draw the other half of this ice-cream sundae.

Fill in the missing vowels.

C H ____ C ____ L ____ T ____

V ____ N ____ L L ____

S T R ____ W B ____ R R Y

R ____ C K Y R ____ ____ D

B ____ B B L ____ G ____ M

Analogies

Ice cream is to **cold** as **soup** is to _____.

Ice cream is to **cone** as **milk** is to _____.

Sprinkles are to **ice cream** as **icing** is to _____.

Critical and Creative Thinking Activities • EMC 3393 • © Evan-Moor Corp.

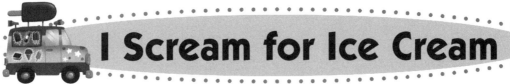
I Scream for Ice Cream

Ice cream is cold. What are 3 other things that are cold?

1. _____ 2. _____ 3. _____

Ice cream melts. What are 3 other things that melt?

1. _____ 2. _____ 3. _____

Ice cream costs $0.75 per scoop. Sprinkles cost $0.35. How much would each of these cost?

1 scoop with sprinkles _____

2 scoops, <u>no</u> sprinkles _____

2 scoops with sprinkles _____

Mom bought a box of 16 ice-cream bars. Jake and his friends ate half of them. Karla and her friends ate half of what was left. Dad ate 2. How many ice-cream bars are left for Mom?

_____ ice-cream bars

What are 3 reasons a person might <u>not</u> want to eat ice cream?

1. _____

2. _____

3. _____

I Scream for Ice Cream

Can you think of 21 different flavors of ice cream?
Write the name of the flavor on each scoop.

   Critical and Creative Thinking Activities • EMC 3393 • © Evan-Moor Corp.

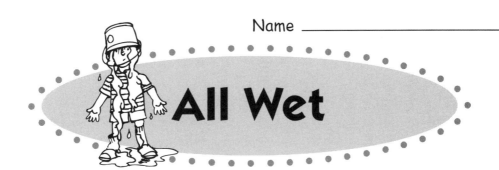

All Wet

What are 10 different things that we use water for?

1. _____

2. _____

3. _____

4. _____

5. _____

6. _____

7. _____

8. _____

9. _____

10. _____

Circle raindrops that add up to **16**. You may circle as many raindrops as you like. Your circles can overlap. One example is done for you.

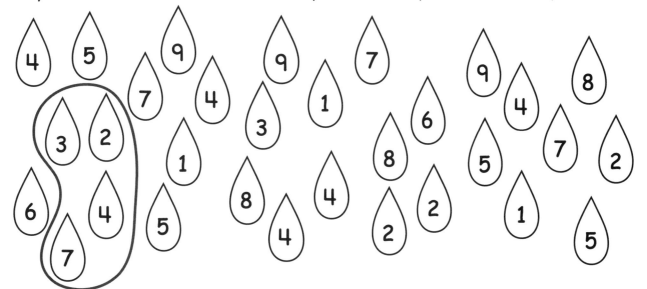

How many groups of 16 did you find? _____

All Wet

Would you rather take a shower or a bath? _____

Why? _____

Splish-splash! Use the clues to find other words that begin with **sp**.

where rockets go   sp_____

to go round and round   sp_____

tipped-over liquid   sp_____

used to eat soup   sp_____

to talk   sp_____

thin pasta   sp_____

Where can you find water in nature?

_____

_____

_____

_____

_____

_____

Unscramble the words to make a sentence.

other   rain   some   come   rain   away   go   day   again

_____

_____

    Critical and Creative Thinking Activities • EMC 3393 • © Evan-Moor Corp.

All Wet

The word **rain** has the letters **r** and **n** in it. How many other words can you make that have both of these letters in them? The **r** <u>must</u> come before the **n**.
Examples: **run**, **grant**

1. _____
2. _____
3. _____
4. _____
5. _____

6. _____
7. _____
8. _____
9. _____
10. _____

11. _____
12. _____
13. _____
14. _____
15. _____

The word **wet** has the letters **w** and **t** in it. See how many other words you can make that have **w** and **t** in them. The **w** <u>must</u> come before the **t**.

1. _____
2. _____
3. _____
4. _____
5. _____

6. _____
7. _____
8. _____
9. _____
10. _____

11. _____
12. _____
13. _____
14. _____
15. _____

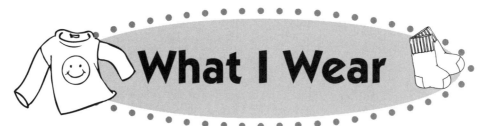

What I Wear

Analogies

Sock is to **foot** as **hat** is to _____.

Shirt is to **washing machine** as **dish** is to _____.

Mitten is to **two** as **glove** is to _____.

Describe the shirt that you are wearing right now. Use as many details as you can. Then draw your shirt in the box.

_____

_____

_____

_____

_____

Grandma knit 3 pairs of socks for each of her grandchildren. She has 14 grandchildren. How many socks did Grandma knit?

_____ socks

What I Wear

What are 3 reasons you might <u>never</u> wear your favorite shirt again?

1. _____

2. _____

3. _____

Change 1 letter in each word to make a type of clothing.

PARTS _____

SHORT _____

PRESS _____

LOCK _____

COAL _____

HAM _____

WEST _____

Short-sleeved shirts cost $6. Long-sleeved shirts cost $9. Shannon bought 7 shirts. She spent $51. How many of each type of shirt did Shannon buy?

_____ short-sleeved shirts

_____ long-sleeved shirts

What I Wear

You get points for what you are wearing! Use the chart to answer the questions. Show your work.

• How many points are you wearing?

_____

• Compare your points with a friend's.

Who has more points? _____

How many more points? _____

How many points do you have altogether?

_____

• Find 2 more people. How many points do all 4 of you have?

_____

• Try to find someone who has the same number of points as you do. Write his or her name.

_____

Item	Points
Shirt	16
Pants or shorts	18
Skirt	18
Dress	15
Socks	6 (each)
Tights or stockings	13
Shoes	7 (each)
Hat	12
Watch	17
Other jewelry	7 (each)
Belt	11
Vest	13
Jacket/sweatshirt	10
Hair clips/bands	14
Braces	19
Glasses	19
Underwear	50

Name _____

Boxes

You find a box about the size of a cat on your doorstep.
What could be inside?

Good things	Bad things

The word **box** ends in **x**.
Read each clue and write
another word that ends in **x**.

to stir   _____x

used for candles   _____x

to make unbroken _____x

one more than 5   _____x

ate the
Gingerbread Man _____x

Group A 3 boxes	Group B 7 boxes
• 1 has $100 inside. • The other 2 are empty.	• 2 have $100 inside. • The other 5 are empty.

• • • • • • • • • • • •

You may open <u>only</u> one box.
Which **group** gives you the best chance
of getting the money?

_____

Boxes

What are 3 things you could use a shoebox for?

1. _____

2. _____

3. _____

Dora received 4 boxes for her birthday. She opened the **yellow** box after the **green** box but before the **blue** box. She opened the **red** box first. Color the boxes in the order that Dora opened them.

You found a mysterious box with a note on it that reads:

"Open this box and your life will change forever."

Will you open the box?

_____

Finish the 3 sentences.

The big box _____.

_____ found a small box _____.

_____ inside the box.

 Critical and Creative Thinking Activities • EMC 3393 • © Evan-Moor Corp.

Boxes

Show 3 different ways to divide the boxes into groups. Each time, write the letters to show the 2 groups you made. Then write the rule that tells how the groups go together.

```
   A      B      C      D      E    F
          G  H   I   J   K   L   M   N
```

Group 1: _____ Group 2: _____

Rule: _____

Group 1: _____ Group 2: _____

Rule: _____

Group 1: _____ Group 2: _____

Rule: _____

Name _____

Pockets

How many pockets are on your clothes right now? _____

Would it be good or bad to have pockets on your socks? _____

Why? _____

Lizzy has 7 marbles in her pocket. 3 of them are blue and 4 of them are red. How many marbles will she have to take out of her pocket to be sure she will get a blue marble?

_____ marbles

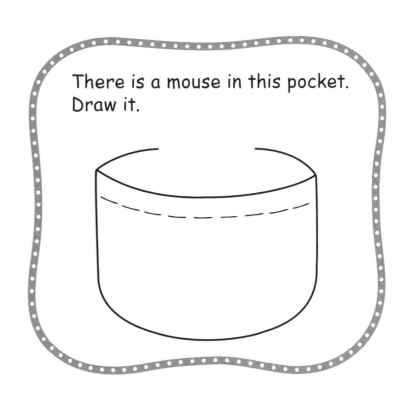

There is a mouse in this pocket. Draw it.

Circle things that you might put in your back pocket. Cross off things that you should probably <u>not</u> put in your back pocket.

comb	pet lizard	scissors
chocolate bar	egg	toy car
pencil	wallet	strawberry

Critical and Creative Thinking Activities • EMC 3393 • © Evan-Moor Corp.

Pockets

What exactly is a pocket?_____

_____

Besides clothing, what is something that has a pocket? _____

How many smaller words can you make from this word:

P O C K E T

1. _____   5. _____

2. _____   6. _____

3. _____   7. _____

4. _____   8. _____

How is a pocket the same as an envelope?

_____

How is a pocket different from an envelope?

_____

Pockets

What are 3 things that each of these people might have in their pockets?

Clown

Dog walker

Teenager

Teacher

8-year-old child

Carpenter

Gardener

Magician

The tooth fairy

Critical and Creative Thinking Activities • EMC 3393 • © Evan-Moor Corp.

Bottles and Jars

Why is peanut butter sold in jars instead of bottles?

_____

Why is soda sold in bottles instead of jars?

_____

There are exactly 14 marbles in this bottle. The bottle is full. Draw the marbles.

Bill has 9 quarters, 15 dimes, 7 nickels, and 19 pennies in a jar.

How many coins? _____

How much money? _____

Write a sentence about bottles. Use exactly 8 words.

_____

_____

Bottles and Jars

What are 3 things that you can do with an empty jar?

1. _____

2. _____

3. _____

Unscramble the letters to make the names of things that come in bottles.

A S O D _____

P E C K U T H _____

V I L E O L I O _____

P E M A L R U S P Y _____

P A L E P C E J U I _____

Each answer rhymes with **jar**.

in the sky _____

not near _____

drive it _____

mark on skin _____

put on roads _____

Unscramble the words to make a sentence.

of   party   bottles   for   bought   seven   the   we   soda

_____

Bottles and Jars

The words listed below name things that can be found in bottles or jars.
Use the words to fill in the puzzle.

4 letters	5 letters	6 letters	7 letters
MILK	~~JELLY~~	OLIVES	COOKIES
NUTS	HONEY	RELISH	KETCHUP
SODA	SYRUP	SPICES	MUSTARD
	WATER		PICKLES
	JUICE		

Paper

What are 4 words that describe this piece of paper?

1. _____   3. _____

2. _____   4. _____

If you were to take this paper and fold it in half and then in half again and then in half one more time and then unfold it, how many boxes would you have made with the fold lines?

_____ boxes

A roll of toilet paper is 350 feet long. How long are...

2 rolls? _____

3 rolls? _____

4 rolls? _____

The answer is **a paper towel**. What is the question?

_____

The answer is **a paper boat**. What is the question?

_____

    Critical and Creative Thinking Activities • EMC 3393 • © Evan-Moor Corp.

Paper

You need to write down a phone number, but you don't have any paper. What can you use instead?

_____

The word **paper** begins with **p** and ends in **r**. Use the clues to make other words that begin with **p** and end in **r**.

a fruit   p_____r

game participant   p_____r

not rich   p_____r

two of a kind   p_____r

The **yellow** paper is under the **red** paper. The **blue** paper is on the top. The **green** paper is between the **blue** and the **red** papers. Color the papers.

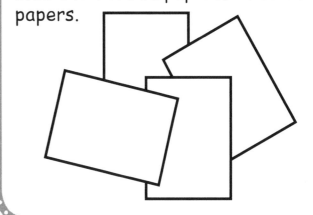

Draw lines to show how you could cut the paper into equal pieces.

      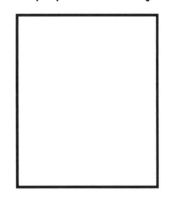   

2 equal pieces   3 equal pieces   4 equal pieces   6 equal pieces

© Evan-Moor Corp. • EMC 3393 • Critical and Creative Thinking Activities

Paper

Answer each clue with the name of something that is made from paper.
Then unscramble the letters in the boxes to complete the sentence
at the bottom of this page.

drink from it ☐ ___ ___

hang this type of picture on the wall ___ ___ ___ ___ ___ ☐

on a bottle or jar ☐ ___ ___ ___ ___

use to blow your nose ☐ ___ ___ ___ ___ ___

eat off it ___ ___ ___ ☐

use to clean up a spill ___ ___ ___ ☐ ___

also called a bag ___ ___ ☐ ___

funny story told in pictures ___ ___ ___ ☐ ___

use to look up words ___ ___ ___ ___ ___ ☐

When you are done with paper, you should

___ ___ ___ ___ ___ ___ ___ ___   ___ ___!

   Critical and Creative Thinking Activities • EMC 3393 • © Evan-Moor Corp.

Cartoons

How many cartoon characters can you name? Use the back if you need more room.

1. _____   4. _____   7. _____

2. _____   5. _____   8. _____

3. _____   6. _____   9. _____

Analogies

Mickey is to mouse as _____ is to duck.

Snoopy is to Charlie Brown as _____ is to Shaggy.

Forest is to Bambi as _____ is to SpongeBob.

What are 3 things that can happen in a cartoon that <u>cannot</u> happen in real life?

1. _____

2. _____

3. _____

Name _____

Cartoons

Do you like movies with cartoons or with real people? _____

Why? _____

_____

Name a cartoon character that is...

funny _____

nice _____

mean _____

clumsy _____

smart_____

cute _____

Mickey Mouse had 34 cookies. He gave 6 cookies each to Goofy, Donald, and Pluto. He gave half of what was left to Minnie Mouse. How many cookies does Mickey have left?

_____ cookies left

If they met, do you think Mickey Mouse and SpongeBob SquarePants would be friends? _____

Why or why not? _____

_____

Cartoons

Create a cartoon character. It can be a person, an animal, or a made-up creature. Draw your character in the box. Then answer the questions.

What is the character's name?

_____

Where does he, she, or it live?

_____

What does he, she, or it do?

_____

_____

_____

Write 6 words that describe this character.

1. _____   4. _____

2. _____   5. _____

3. _____   6. _____

Listen!

This is a quiet line.

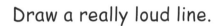

This line is a little louder.

Draw a really loud line.

The town clock marks the hours with bells—1 chime for 1:00, 2 chimes for 2:00, and so on, until 12:00. How many times altogether will the clock bells chime in 12 hours?

_____ chimes

What are 3 things that you would hear...

in a forest?   _____ _____ _____

at a ballgame?   _____ _____ _____

at a bowling alley? _____ _____ _____

Analogies

Ring is to **phone** as _____ is to **horn**.

Loud is to **shout** as _____ is to **whisper**.

Clap is to **hands** as _____ is to **feet**.

Name _____

What are 3 things that you would <u>not</u> be able to do if you could not hear?

1. _____

2. _____

3. _____

When is it good to whisper, and when is it good to shout?

Whisper	Shout

What is the loudest noise that you can think of? _____

What is the softest noise that you can still hear? _____

What is a sound that you like to hear? _____

What is a sound that you do <u>not</u> like to hear? _____

Listen!

When a word sounds like what it is describing, it is called **onomatopoeia**.
What sounds do the words below describe?

squeak _____

trickle _____

slurp _____

crash _____

pop _____

Write a word that sounds like the description.

a bee _____   a tomato hitting a wall _____

a phone _____   breaking glass _____

a cannon _____   eating an apple _____

a fire _____   horse hooves _____

Write a sentence that uses onomatopoeia.

_____

_____

On the Screen

Oh dear! All of the screens in your house have stopped working.
No more TV, computer, or video games! What can you do instead?

1. _____   5. _____

2. _____   6. _____

3. _____   7. _____

4. _____   8. _____

Why do you think the keys on a computer keyboard are <u>not</u>
in alphabetical order?

_____

_____

Jessica woke up at 7:30 on Saturday morning. She watched cartoons for two and a half hours. What time was it when Jessica turned off the TV? _____	Carlos uses the computer every day from 3:00 to 4:30. How many hours does he use the computer each week? _____ hours

Would you rather rent a movie or go to a movie in a theater? _____

Why? _____

On the Screen

What do people use computers for?

1. _____   5. _____

2. _____   6. _____

3. _____   7. _____

4. _____   8. _____

Most American children watch about 3 hours of television every day. How many hours of TV are watched in a week?

_____ hours a week

About how many hours of TV do you watch…

in a day? _____

in a week? _____

What does this say?

I M

_____

T V

_____

Do you think you watch too much TV? _____

Why or why not? _____

   Critical and Creative Thinking Activities • EMC 3393 • © Evan-Moor Corp.

 On the Screen

Tina, **Jimmy**, **Molly**, **Adam**, **Maya**, and **Will** each like a different
TV show. Read the clues, and then write the name of each person
next to his or her favorite show.
Hint: You will need to read the clues at least 2 times.

- **Jimmy** and **Tina** do <u>not</u> like shows with animals.

- **Molly's** show has 4 words in its title.

- None of the girls like *Bowling with the Stars*.

- None of the boys like *The Wonderful World of Worms*.

- **Will** wants to be a teacher when he grows up.

_____ *The Wonderful World of Worms*

_____ *American Teacher*

_____ *Bowling with the Stars*

_____ *Ponies on Ice*

_____ *Everybody Loves Paper Clips*

_____ *Science with the President*

Lost and Found

What should you do if you've lost...

your homework? _____

your coat? _____

your dog? _____

Number these things that can be lost from 1 to 6. The one that would be the <u>worst</u> to lose should be number 1.

_____ your reading glasses

_____ your coat

_____ your lunch

_____ your pencil

_____ the TV remote

_____ your pet

Tom, **Brian**, and **Doug** each lost something. Brian and Doug did <u>not</u> lose hats. Doug <u>never</u> wears a scarf. Who lost each of these things?

mittens _____

hat _____

scarf _____

What is the most important thing that you have ever lost?

_____

 Critical and Creative Thinking Activities • EMC 3393 • © Evan-Moor Corp.

Name _____

Lost and Found

You have found a dollar on the playground. What do you do?

_____

You get lost in a store. What should you do?

_____

Marshall, Will, and Holly have each lost their way home. Trace each of their paths with a different color.

In a game of hide-and-seek, do you like to hide or to seek? _____

Why? _____

Name _____

Lost and Found

Penny has lost her lucky socks. Help her find them by unscrambling the places she has already looked. Then write the letters from the boxes in order on the lines at the bottom of this page to find the answer.

Penny has already looked in these places:

in her OLDLSOEUH __ __ __ [ ] __ __ __ __ __

under the EDB __ [ ] __

behind the OROD __ __ __ [ ]

in her PRESLISP __ __ __ __ [ ] __ __ __

in her GYGIP KBAN __ [ ] __ __ __   __ __ __ __

at the back of her SCETOL __ [ ] __ __ __ __

behind the LKSOFEBHO __ __ __ __ [ ] __ __ __ __

in her YTO XBO __ [ ] __   __ __ __

in her desk WREDAR __ __ __ [ ] __ __

Penny finally found her lucky socks under

__ __ __ __   __ __ __ __ __ __ __ !

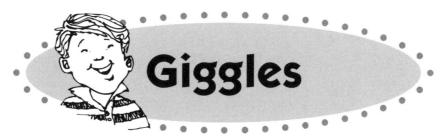

Giggles

Finish each sentence.

I always laugh when _____.

Giggling is embarrassing when _____.

Laughing can hurt someone's feelings when _____

_____.

The word **giggles** is full of **g**'s. Use the clues to find other words that have more than one **g**.

to choke   G ___ G

leaving   G ___ ___ ___ G

suitcases   B ___ G G ___ G E

Internet search   G ___ ___ G ___ ___

really big   G ___ G ___ ___ ___ ___ ___

wear while
swimming   G ___ G G ___ ___ ___

Keri went to see a funny movie. The movie was 1 hour and 32 minutes long. It ended at 3:42. At what time did the movie start?

_____

Keri bought popcorn for $3.25. She paid with a $10 bill. How much change did she get back?

$_____

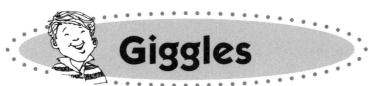

Giggles

What are 3 things that make you giggle?

1. _____

2. _____

3. _____

Name a funny...

movie _____

book _____

TV show _____

person _____

What is another word for...

giggle _____

smile _____

funny _____

happy _____

What would make a 2-year-old child giggle but would <u>not</u> make you giggle?

_____

What makes you giggle now but probably <u>won't</u> when you are an adult?

_____

 Critical and Creative Thinking Activities • EMC 3393 • © Evan-Moor Corp.

Giggles

Can you solve these silly story problems?

Katie ate 26 beetles for breakfast. Then she ate 57 ants for lunch and 37 grasshoppers for dinner. How many bugs did Katie eat altogether?

_____ bugs

Elliot had 17 pairs of socks in his dirty sock collection. His sister gave him 19 more pairs of dirty socks. How many socks does Elliot have now?

_____ dirty socks

Jody found 33 slugs. She put them under her pillow for the Slug Fairy. The Slug Fairy took 17 of them and left Jody a box of frozen spinach. How many slugs does Jody have left?

_____ slugs

Arnold has made a super-charged robot that can chew gum and blow really big bubbles. The robot needs 12 volts of electricity to work. Arnold's batteries each have 1.5 volts of electricity. How many batteries does Arnold's robot need?

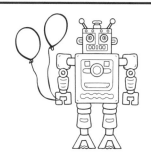

_____ batteries

Name _____

Analogies

Night is to **dark** as **day** is to _____.

Night is to **moon** as **day** is to _____.

Night is to **sleep** as **day** is to _____.

What are 3 things that you can do to help yourself fall asleep?

1. _____

2. _____

3. _____

Each night, Katie reads 8 pages before she goes to sleep. If it takes her 3 minutes to read a page, how long does Katie read each night?

_____ minutes

Katie is reading a book that has 92 pages. If she reads 8 pages each night, how many nights will it take Katie to finish the book?

_____ nights

  Critical and Creative Thinking Activities • EMC 3393 • © Evan-Moor Corp.

Nighttime

What do you think is the perfect bedtime for a child your age? _____

Why? _____

_____

It is nighttime. You are in bed. What do you hear?

_____

_____

_____

_____

Animals that sleep during the day and come out at night are called **nocturnal**. Can you think of 3 nocturnal animals?

1. _____

2. _____

3. _____

What are 3 ways your life would be different if people were nocturnal?

1. _____

2. _____

3. _____

Name _____

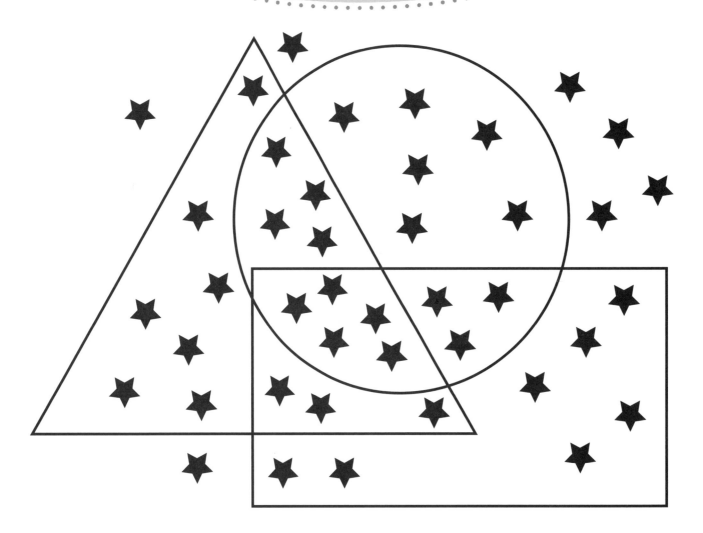

How many stars are in the shapes?

triangle only _____   triangle and circle _____

rectangle only _____   triangle and rectangle _____

circle only _____   all three shapes _____

circle and rectangle _____   no shapes _____

My Birthday

When is your birthday?

_____

Do you think it is better to have a birthday in the fall, winter, spring, or summer?

_____

Why? _____

How many months old will you be on your next birthday? Remember, there are 12 months in a year.

_____ months

How many weeks old will you be on your next birthday? Remember, there are 52 weeks in a year.

_____ weeks

Write a sentence about your birthday. Use exactly 8 words.

_____

_____

My Birthday

Fill in the missing vowels for these **birthday** words.

C __ K __   G __ M __ S

PR __ S __ NTS   __ C __ CR __ __ M

P __ RTY H __ TS   C __ NDL __ S

B __ LL __ __ NS   __ NV __ T __ T __ __ NS

How many words can you make with the letters in this word?

BIRTHDAY

1. _____

2. _____

3. _____

4. _____

5. _____

6. _____

This is your birthday cake. Decorate it!

My Birthday

What did Risa get for her birthday? For each clue, find the letter that is in the first boldfaced word but <u>not</u> in the second boldfaced word. Then write those letters in order on the lines in the box below to find out what Risa got.

- It is in **REACH** but not in **CHEER**.

- It is in **CABLE** but not in **LACE**.

- It is in **BITE** but not in **BEET**.

- It is in **CLOSE** but not in **LOSER**.

- It is in **TODAY** but not in **TOAD**.

- It is in **RACK** but not in **RAKE**.

- It is in **LIFT** but not in **FIGHT**.

- It is in **TRADE** but not in **DART**.

Risa got

____ _____ ___ ____ ____ ____ ____ ____.

What are 3 presents that you would like to get for your birthday?

1. _____   2. _____   3. _____

Name _____

Homework

About how much time do you think a child your age should spend on homework each day?

_____ Why do you think so? _____

_____

About how much time do you spend on homework each day? _____

_____

What kind of homework did Juan get? Cross out the letters of the kinds of homework he did <u>not</u> get to find the kind he <u>did</u> get.

G E Z S M I S L N A P E I U T E C N H L I C Q

He did <u>not</u> get **SPELLING**.

He did <u>not</u> get **SCIENCE**.

He did <u>not</u> have to study for a **QUIZ**.

Juan's homework was

_____.

The answer is **my homework**. What is the question?

_____

Critical and Creative Thinking Activities • EMC 3393 • © Evan-Moor Corp.

Homework

Why do teachers give homework? List 2 reasons.

1. _____

2. _____

Marta eats a snack before she does her homework. She feeds her cat after she goes to soccer practice. She does her homework before soccer practice. Write the order of Marta's activities.

First: _____

Second: _____

Third: _____

Fourth: _____

Number these places where you could do your homework from 1 to 5. The one that would be the best place should be number 1.

_____ in your room

_____ at a bowling alley

_____ at the kitchen table

_____ in a treehouse

_____ at the library

If you could give your teacher homework for tonight, what assignment would you give?

_____

_____

Name _____

Homework

Calvin did his homework, but he got a lot of the problems wrong.
Correct his paper. Circle the problems he got wrong, and draw a star
by the ones he got right. Then write a score at the top of the paper.

Name: **Calvin**

Add:

¹34 +17 = **51**	¹26 +57 = **83**	¹35 +48 = **84**	21 +39 = **50**

$$\begin{array}{r} {\scriptstyle 1} \\ 34 \\ +17 \\ \hline 51 \end{array} \qquad \begin{array}{r} {\scriptstyle 1} \\ 26 \\ +57 \\ \hline 83 \end{array} \qquad \begin{array}{r} {\scriptstyle 1} \\ 35 \\ +48 \\ \hline 84 \end{array} \qquad \begin{array}{r} \\ 21 \\ +39 \\ \hline 50 \end{array}$$

$$\begin{array}{r} {\scriptstyle 1} \\ 63 \\ +18 \\ \hline 81 \end{array} \qquad \begin{array}{r} {\scriptstyle 1} \\ 45 \\ +28 \\ \hline 72 \end{array} \qquad \begin{array}{r} {\scriptstyle 1} \\ 55 \\ +36 \\ \hline 91 \end{array} \qquad \begin{array}{r} \\ 18 \\ +45 \\ \hline 53 \end{array}$$

$$\begin{array}{r} \\ 53 \\ +24 \\ \hline 32 \end{array} \qquad \begin{array}{r} {\scriptstyle 1} \\ 67 \\ +17 \\ \hline 84 \end{array} \qquad \begin{array}{r} {\scriptstyle 1} \\ 26 \\ +65 \\ \hline 91 \end{array} \qquad \begin{array}{r} {\scriptstyle 2} \\ 43 \\ +29 \\ \hline 81 \end{array}$$

Critical and Creative Thinking Activities • EMC 3393 • © Evan-Moor Corp.

Books

Do you like to read? _____

Why or why not? _____

Think about the books that you have read or have had read to you. Which one was the...

funniest? _____

scariest? _____

longest? _____

Taylor got 12 books from the library. One-third of them were about birds. One-fourth of them were about cats. The rest were about monkeys. How many of the books were about monkeys?

_____ monkey books

Which kinds of books have you read? Write **R** for the ones you have read. Write **N** for the ones you have <u>not</u> read.

_____ chapter books

_____ picture books

_____ comic books

_____ animal books

_____ biographies

_____ science books

_____ manga

_____ joke books

_____ fantasy books

_____ nonfiction books

Books

How are a bookstore and a library the same and different? List 3 ways for each.

Same	Different

What is the name of the last book that you read? _____

Write a fact about the last book that you read.

_____

Write an opinion about the last book that you read.

_____

Analogies

Book is to **shelf** as **sock** is to _____.

Book is to **read** as **music** is to _____.

Book is to **author** as **painting** is to _____.

 Critical and Creative Thinking Activities • EMC 3393 • © Evan-Moor Corp.

Books

Each of these 6 children is reading a different book. Read the clues.
Then write the child's name next to his or her book.
Hint: You will need to read the clues at least 2 times.

- **Meredith** and **Ramon** both chose books about dogs.

- **Christina** will need special materials in order to use her book.

- **George's** book is about mythical creatures.

- **Derek's** book is <u>not</u> about animals.

- None of the girls chose a book with the number **101** in the title.

> Meredith
> George
> Izzie
> Ramon
> Christina
> Derek

_____

_____

_____

_____

_____

_____

© Evan-Moor Corp. • EMC 3393 • Critical and Creative Thinking Activities

Cents Sense

The answer is **a quarter**. What is the question?

_____

The answer is **two nickels**. What is the question?

_____

Would you rather have:

22 nickels **or** 12 dimes?

22 nickels **or** 5 quarters?

15 dimes **or** 5 quarters?

Write **cent**, **sent**, or **scent**.

a letter _____

a flower _____

a penny _____

Put these coins in order from the oldest to the newest.

2004   **1999**   **2003**   **2007**   **1992**   **1995**   **2001**

____   ____   ____   ____   ____   ____   ____

    Critical and Creative Thinking Activities • EMC 3393 • © Evan-Moor Corp.

Cents Sense

Pretend that you have 1,000 pennies. What are 3 things that you could do with them besides spending them?

1. _____

2. _____

3. _____

Analogies

Quarter is to circle as dollar bill is to _____.

Dime is to silver as penny is to _____.

Penny is to 1¢ as nickel is to _____.

A new $0.75 coin is being made. You get to design it!

Who will be on the front?

_____

What will be on the back?

_____

Draw the two sides of the new coin.

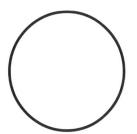
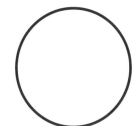

What will the coin be called?

_____

© Evan-Moor Corp. • EMC 3393 • Critical and Creative Thinking Activities

Cents Sense

Each piggy bank shows the amount of money and the number of coins that are inside. Use letters to tell which coins are in each piggy bank.
Hint: You may want to use real coins.

| P = Penny |
| N = Nickel |
| D = Dime |
| Q = Quarter |

$0.17
5 coins

_____

$0.33
7 coins

_____

$0.61
6 coins

_____

$0.90
8 coins

_____

Critical and Creative Thinking Activities • EMC 3393 • © Evan-Moor Corp.

Answer Key

Many of the questions in this book are open-ended, and students' answers will vary. Sample responses are provided for most of these activities. Accept any reasonable responses.

Page 5

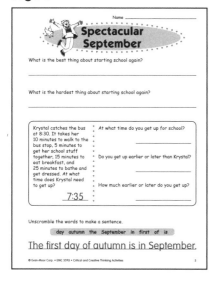

Page 6

Page 7

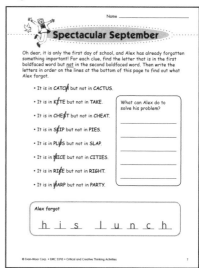

Page 8

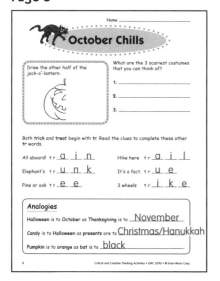

Page 9

Page 10

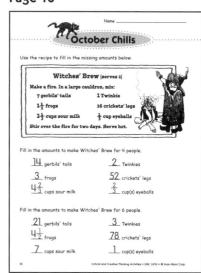

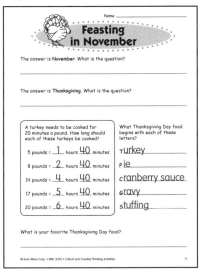

Name _____

Feasting in November

The answer is **November**. What is the question?
_____

The answer is **Thanksgiving**. What is the question?
_____

A turkey needs to be cooked for 20 minutes a pound. How long should each of these turkeys be cooked?

5 pounds __1__ hours __40__ minutes

8 pounds __2__ hours __40__ minutes

14 pounds __4__ hours __40__ minutes

17 pounds __5__ hours __40__ minutes

20 pounds __6__ hours __40__ minutes

What is your favorite Thanksgiving Day food?
_____

What Thanksgiving Day food begins with each of these letters?

T urkey

P ie

C ranberry sauce

G ravy

stuffing

Name _____

Feasting in November

Number these things from 1 to 6. The thing you are most thankful for should be number 1.

___ food

___ friends

___ toys

___ education

___ family

___ video games

You are making Thanksgiving dinner, but you <u>cannot</u> make turkey, mashed potatoes, or any of the usual Thanksgiving Day foods. What will you make?
_____

Thanksgiving is always on the 4th Thursday in November. Read each clue about another holiday, and then write its name.

• the last day of the tenth month   Halloween

• the 4th day of the seventh month   Independence Day

• the 17th of a month that begins with M   St. Patrick's Day

• the 14th of a month that begins with F   Valentine's Day

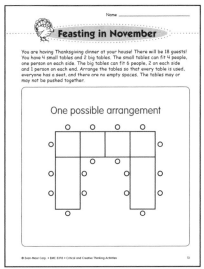

Name _____

Feasting in November

You are having Thanksgiving dinner at your house! There will be 18 guests! You have 4 small tables and 2 big tables. The small tables can fit 4 people, one person on each side. The big tables can fit 6 people, 2 on each side and 1 person on each end. Arrange the tables so that every table is used, everyone has a seat, and there are no empty spaces. The tables may or may not be pushed together.

One possible arrangement

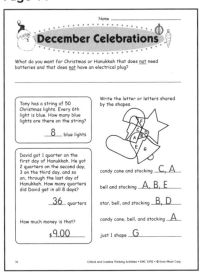

Name _____

December Celebrations

What do you want for Christmas or Hanukkah that does <u>not</u> need batteries and that does <u>not</u> have an electrical plug?
_____

Tony has a string of 50 Christmas lights. Every 6th light is blue. How many blue lights are there on the string?

__8__ blue lights

David got 1 quarter on the first day of Hanukkah. He got 2 quarters on the second day, 3 on the third day, and so on, through the last day of Hanukkah. How many quarters did David get in all 8 days?

__36__ quarters

How much money is that?

$__9.00__

Write the letter or letters shared by the shapes.

candy cane and stocking __C, A__

bell and stocking __A, B, E__

star, bell, and stocking __B, D__

candy cane, bell, and stocking __A__

just 1 shape __G__

Name _____

December Celebrations

Describe Christmas or Hanukkah in 1 sentence. _____

Circle 5 things that you would <u>most</u> like to find in your stocking.

candy cane   comic book

bouncy ball   card game

stuffed animal   socks

chocolate Santa   yo-yo

spinning top   mittens

Add 2 more to the list.

Frosty the Snowman

Silent Night

Santa Claus Is Coming to Town

_____

_____

If you could give the same gift to every child in the world, what would you give?
_____

Why? _____

Name _____

December Celebrations

Color the grid to find the hidden picture.

Green tree; colored ornaments as shown; brown trunk.

F5 = green
G9, H9 = green
E4 = red
H1 = green
H6 = green
A5 = yellow
F2–F4 = green
H8 = green
E8, F8, G8 = green
G5 = yellow
E2, E3 = green

C5, C6 = green
B4–B6 = green
C7, D7 = green
I5 = brown
G3, G4 = green
D4, D5 = green
G7 = green
H2 = green
F6, G6 = green
E4 = red
E7 = blue

H7 = green
H3–H5 = green
D3 = green
G2 = blue
F7 = green
C3 = green
G1 = green
D6 = yellow
C4 = blue
E5, E6 = green

Name _____

January Is #1!

It's a new year! What year is it?   **Answers depend on current year**

What year will it be in 25 years? _____   How old will you be? _____

Analogies

January is to month as Sunday is to **day**

January is to winter as July is to **summer**

January is to February as May is to **June**

This year...

I want to go to _____

I want to try _____

I want to learn _____

I <u>don't</u> want to _____

I hope _____

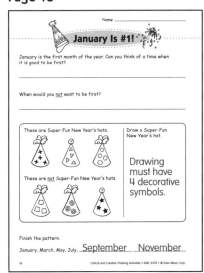

Name _____

January Is #1!

January is the first month of the year. Can you think of a time when it is good to be first?
_____

When would you <u>not</u> want to be first?
_____

These are Super-Fun New Year's hats.

These are <u>not</u> Super-Fun New Year's hats.

Draw a Super-Fun New Year's hat.

Drawing must have 4 decorative symbols.

Finish the pattern.

January, March, May, July, __September__ __November__

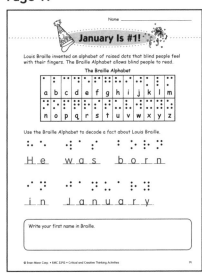

Name _____

January Is #1!

Louis Braille invented an alphabet of raised dots that blind people feel with their fingers. The Braille Alphabet allows blind people to read.

The Braille Alphabet

a b c d e f g h i j k l m

n o p q r s t u v w x y z

Use the Braille Alphabet to decode a fact about Louis Braille.

He was born

in January

Write your first name in Braille.

Critical and Creative Thinking Activities • EMC 3393 • © Evan-Moor Corp.

Page 20

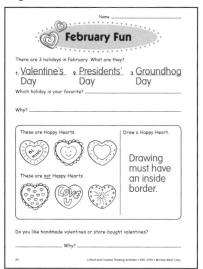

February Fun

Name _____

There are 3 holidays in February. What are they?

1. **Valentine's** Day 2. **Presidents'** Day 3. **Groundhog** Day

Which holiday is your favorite? _____

Why? _____

These are Happy Hearts.

Draw a Happy Heart.

Drawing must have an inside border.

These are **not** Happy Hearts.

Do you like handmade valentines or store-bought valentines?

_____ Why? _____

Page 21

February Fun

Name _____

Write 4 words to describe the weather right now.

1. _____ 3. _____

2. _____ 4. _____

How many mistakes can you find on this calendar? Circle them.

February

SUNDAE	MONDAY	WEDNESDAY	TUESDAY	THURSDAY	FRIDAY	SATURDAY
		0	1	2	3	4
5	6	7	ate	9	10	11
12	13	14	15	16	17	18
14	16	15	17	18		
19	20	21	22	23	24	24
26	27	28	29	30		

How many mistakes did you find? __17__

Presidents' Day is in February. If you were the president, what would you do?

_____

Page 22

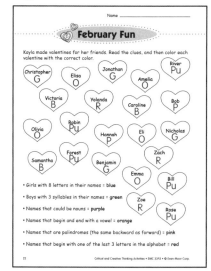

February Fun

Name _____

Kayla made valentines for her friends. Read the clues, and then color each valentine with the correct color.

Christopher G, Elisa O, Jonathan G, Amelia O, River Pu

Victoria B, Yolanda R, Caroline B, Bob P

Olivia O, Robin Pu, Hannah P, Eli O, Nicholas G

Samantha B, Forest Pu, Benjamin G, Zach R, Emma O, Bill Pu

Zoe R, Rose Pu

- Girls with 8 letters in their names = blue
- Boys with 3 syllables in their names = green
- Names that could be nouns = purple
- Names that begin and end with a vowel = orange
- Names that are palindromes (the same backward as forward) = pink
- Names that begin with one of the last 3 letters in the alphabet = red

Page 23

Marvelous March

Name _____

Read the statement about March. Write A if it is **always** true. Write S if it is **sometimes** true. Write N if it is **never** true.

__A__ There are 31 days. __S__ It is windy.

__S__ It rains. __S__ I wear sandals.

__S__ I wear green. __N__ I go trick-or-treating.

The first day of spring is in March. What signs of spring can you see?

_____

Draw a leprechaun. He must be wearing a hat and must be smiling. Write what he is thinking.

Leprechaun must be wearing a hat and smiling.

Page 24

Marvelous March

Name _____

It is said that leprechauns bring good luck. What do you think these phrases about luck mean?

"Lucky break" _____

"Lucky charm" _____

"Dumb luck" _____

Complete the 2-word phrases. Each word **must** begin with the same letter. The first word **must** be an adjective. The second word **must** be a noun.
Example: **Marvelous March**

_____ snake

_____ doughnuts

Green _____

Big _____

Add 2 more to the list.

shamrock

broccoli

EXIT sign

leaf

Would you rather be a leprechaun, an elf, or a fairy? _____

Why? _____

Page 25

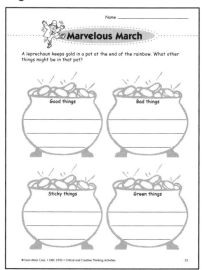

Marvelous March

Name _____

A leprechaun keeps gold in a pot at the end of the rainbow. What other things might be in that pot?

Good things

Bad things

Sticky things

Green things

Page 26

April Surprises

Name _____

The lunch ladies played an April Fools' Day joke on the students by scrambling the menu. Unscramble the words to see what is for lunch.

HENKCIC STENUGG **chicken nuggets**

LYFFFU CERI **fluffy rice**

ERGEN SNABE **green beans**

LOCOTEACH PIGDUND **chocolate pudding**

PALEP CEIJU **apple juice**

Look carefully. What do the unscrambled words have in common?

_____

Is it okay to tell a lie on April Fools' Day if it is part of a joke? _____

Why or why not? _____

Page 27

April Surprises

Name _____

nac uoy etirw ruoy eman sdrawkcab?
Can you write your name backwards?

woh tuoba ruoy s'rehcoet eman?
How about your teacher's name?

etirw a s'dneirf eman sdrawkcab.
Write a friend's name backwards.

Sydney found 24 eggs in 4 different colors.

- One-third of the eggs were purple.
- She found one less green egg than the number of purple eggs.
- There were twice as many pink eggs as yellow eggs.

How many did Sydney find of each?

__8__ purple eggs

__7__ green eggs

__6__ pink eggs

__3__ yellow eggs

Which egg is different?

Page 28

April Surprises

Name _____

On April 1, David could **not** find any socks to wear! In his empty sock drawer, he found a mysterious note in code. To crack the code, read each letter, and then write the letter that comes just before it in the alphabet.
Example: B = A

Z P V S   T P D L T
Your   socks

B S F   J O   U I F
are   in   the

G S F F A F S   I B Q Q Z
freezer!   Happy

B Q S J M   G P P M T   E B Z
April   Fools'   Day!

Page 29

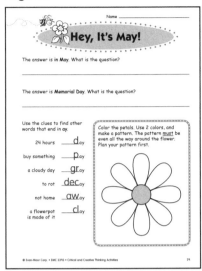

Name _____

Hey, It's May!

The answer is **in May**. What is the question?

_____

The answer is **Memorial Day**. What is the question?

_____

Use the clues to find other words that end in ay.

24 hours	d_ay
buy something	p_ay
a cloudy day	gr_ay
to rot	dec_ay
not home	aw_ay
a flowerpot is made of it	cl_ay

Color the petals. Use 2 colors, and make a pattern. The pattern **must** be even all the way around the flower. Plan your pattern first.

© Evan-Moor Corp. • EMC 3393 • Critical and Creative Thinking Activities

Page 30

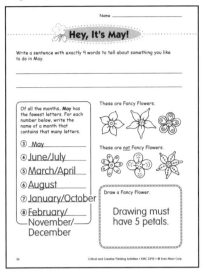

Name _____

Hey, It's May!

Write a sentence with exactly 9 words to tell about something you like to do in May.

_____

Of all the months, **May** has the fewest letters. For each number below, write the name of a month that contains that many letters.

③ May
④ June/July
⑤ March/April
⑥ August
⑦ January/October
⑧ February/November/December

These are Fancy Flowers.

These are **not** Fancy Flowers.

Draw a Fancy Flower.

Drawing must have 5 petals.

Critical and Creative Thinking Activities • EMC 3393 • © Evan-Moor Corp.

Page 31

Name _____

Hey, It's May!

Here is an old saying: "April showers bring May flowers." To complete the name of each flower below, write the letter from the rain cloud in the raindrop. You may use each letter **only** once, so cross them out as you go. Then unscramble the remaining letters in the cloud to make the name of another flower. Write it on the line.

A B C D E E F I L L L M N N O O O P R S S U W Y

R O S E   V I O L E T
L I L Y   P O P P Y
T U L I P   B U T T E R C U P
D A I S Y   D A N D E L I O N
P A N S Y   C A R N A T I O N

The name of another flower is sunflower

© Evan-Moor Corp. • EMC 3393 • Critical and Creative Thinking Activities

Page 32

Name _____

Jazzed About June

What was the most important thing that happened this school year?

_____

How many days of school are left before summer break?

_____

How many hours? _____

When Paris cleaned out her desk at the end of the year, she found 3 quarters, 6 dimes, 5 nickels, and 16 pennies. How much money did Paris find?

$1.76

Think about how you did in school this past year. If you improved in it, draw 1 star by it. If you improved a lot, draw 2 stars by it!

math	following directions
writing	computer skills
spelling	keeping things organized
reading	getting along with others
sports	completing work on time

© Evan-Moor Corp. • EMC 3393 • Critical and Creative Thinking Activities

Page 33

Name _____

Jazzed About June

Complete the 3 sentences about summer.

I want to _____

I **don't** want to _____

I hope _____

Analogies

June is to **summer** as September is to fall

June is to May as November is to October

June is to 6 as January is to 1

Next school year, someone else will sit at your desk. Give 3 pieces of advice to that person about being a student in this classroom.

1. _____
2. _____
3. _____

© Evan-Moor Corp. • EMC 3393 • Critical and Creative Thinking Activities

Page 34

Name _____

Jazzed About June

Circle one of the choices for each question. Then write why you chose it.

Would you rather cool off in a **pool** or in a **lake**?

_____

Would you rather spend a day in the **woods** or at the **beach**?

_____

Would you rather see a **parade** or a **baseball game**?

_____

Would you rather **go camping with your family** for a week or **go away to a kids' camp** for a week?

_____

Critical and Creative Thinking Activities • EMC 3393 • © Evan-Moor Corp.

Page 35

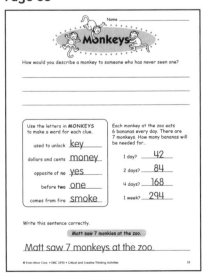

Name _____

Monkeys

How would you describe a monkey to someone who has never seen one?

_____

Use the letters in **MONKEYS** to make a word for each clue.

used to unlock	key
dollars and cents	money
opposite of no	yes
before two	one
comes from fire	smoke

Each monkey at the zoo eats 6 bananas every day. There are 7 monkeys. How many bananas will be needed for...

1 day? 42
2 days? 84
4 days? 168
1 week? 294

Write this sentence correctly.

Matt saw 7 monkeys at the zoo.

Matt saw 7 monkeys at the zoo.

© Evan-Moor Corp. • EMC 3393 • Critical and Creative Thinking Activities

Page 36

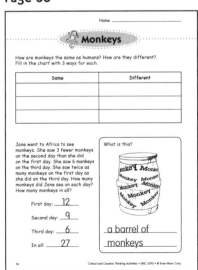

Name _____

Monkeys

How are monkeys the same as humans? How are they different? Fill in the chart with 3 ways for each.

Same	Different

Jane went to Africa to see monkeys. She saw 3 fewer monkeys on the second day than she did on the first day. She saw 6 more monkeys on the third day. She saw twice as many monkeys on the first day as she did on the third day. How many monkeys did Jane see on each day? How many monkeys in all?

First day: 12
Second day: 9
Third day: 6
In all: 27

What is this?

a barrel of monkeys

Critical and Creative Thinking Activities • EMC 3393 • © Evan-Moor Corp.

Page 37

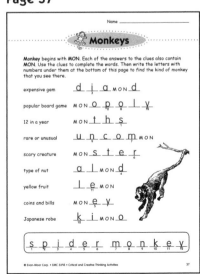

Name _____

Monkeys

Monkey begins with **MON**. Each of the answers to the clues also contain **MON**. Use the clues to complete the words. Then write the letters with numbers under them at the bottom of this page to find the kind of monkey that you see there.

expensive gem	d i a m o n d
popular board game	M O N o p o l y
12 in a year	m o n t h s
rare or unusual	u n c o m m o n
scary creature	M O N s t e r
type of nut	a l m o n d
yellow fruit	l e m o n
coins and bills	M O N e y
Japanese robe	k i m o n o

s p i d e r   m o n k e y

© Evan-Moor Corp. • EMC 3393 • Critical and Creative Thinking Activities

Critical and Creative Thinking Activities • EMC 3393 • © Evan-Moor Corp.

Page 38

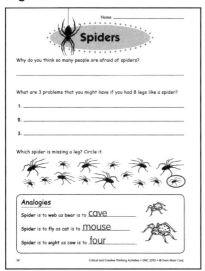

Spiders

Why do you think so many people are afraid of spiders?

What are 3 problems that you might have if you had 8 legs like a spider?

1. _____
2. _____
3. _____

Which spider is missing a leg? Circle it.

Analogies

Spider is to web as bear is to **cave**

Spider is to fly as cat is to **mouse**

Spider is to eight as cow is to **four**

Page 39

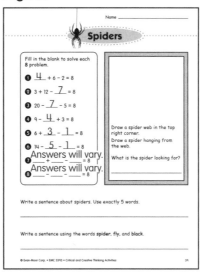

Spiders

Fill in the blank to solve each 8 problem.

1. **4** + 6 − 2 = 8
2. 3 + 12 − **7** = 8
3. 20 − **7** − 5 = 8
4. 9 − **4** + 3 = 8
5. 6 + **3** − **1** = 8
6. 14 − **5** − **1** = 8
7. __ + __ − __ = 8   **Answers will vary.**
8. __ − __ − __ = 8   **Answers will vary.**

Draw a spider web in the top right corner.
Draw a spider hanging from the web.

What is the spider looking for?

Write a sentence about spiders. Use exactly 5 words.

Write a sentence using the words spider, fly, and black.

Page 40

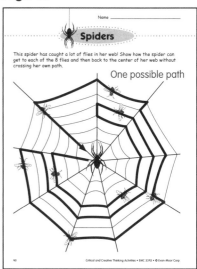

Spiders

This spider has caught a lot of flies in her web! Show how the spider can get to each of the 8 flies and then back to the center of her web without crossing her own path.

One possible path

Page 41

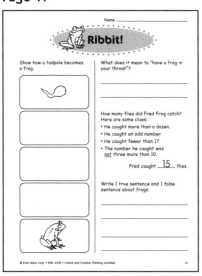

Ribbit!

Show how a tadpole becomes a frog.

What does it mean to "have a frog in your throat"?

How many flies did Fred Frog catch? Here are some clues:
• He caught more than a dozen.
• He caught an odd number.
• He caught fewer than 17.
• The number he caught was not three more than 10.

Fred caught **15** flies.

Write 1 true sentence and 1 false sentence about frogs.

Page 42

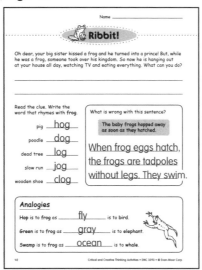

Ribbit!

Oh dear, your big sister kissed a frog and he turned into a prince! But, while he was a frog, someone took over his kingdom. So now he is hanging out at your house all day, watching TV and eating everything. What can you do?

Read the clue. Write the word that rhymes with frog.

pig **hog**

poodle **dog**

dead tree **log**

slow run **jog**

wooden shoe **clog**

What is wrong with this sentence?

The baby frogs hopped away as soon as they hatched.

When frog eggs hatch, the frogs are tadpoles without legs. They swim.

Analogies

Hop is to frog as **fly** is to bird.

Green is to frog as **gray** is to elephant.

Swamp is to frog as **ocean** is to whale.

Page 43

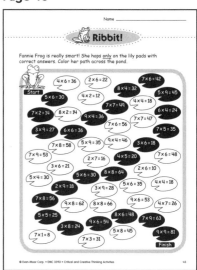

Ribbit!

Fannie Frog is really smart! She hops only on the lily pads with correct answers. Color her path across the pond.

Start
4 × 6 = 36   2 × 6 = 22   7 × 6 = 42
5 × 6 = 30   4 × 2 = 12   8 × 4 = 32   5 × 9 = 45
7 × 2 = 14   8 × 2 = 14   7 × 7 = 49   4 × 4 = 18   6 × 4 = 24
3 × 9 = 27   6 × 6 = 36   7 × 6 = 36   7 × 7 = 47   7 × 5 = 35
7 × 8 = 58   5 × 9 = 35   9 × 4 = 46   3 × 6 = 18
7 × 9 = 53   2 × 7 = 16   4 × 5 = 20   7 × 6 = 48
5 × 4 = 30   3 × 6 = 21   5 × 6 = 30   8 × 8 = 64   2 × 6 = 10
2 × 9 = 18   3 × 9 = 28   6 × 5 = 35   4 × 4 = 12
7 × 8 = 56   9 × 8 = 62   8 × 8 = 66   9 × 6 = 53   4 × 7 = 26
5 × 5 = 25   9 × 6 = 54   8 × 6 = 48   7 × 9 = 63
7 × 1 = 8   3 × 8 = 24   9 × 6 = 50   5 × 8 = 45   9 × 9 = 81
7 × 3 = 31   Finish

Page 44

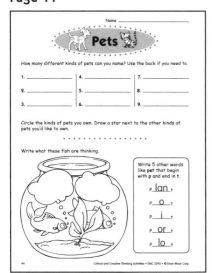

Pets

How many different kinds of pets can you name? Use the back if you need to.

1. ___ 4. ___ 7. ___
2. ___ 5. ___ 8. ___
3. ___ 6. ___ 9. ___

Circle the kinds of pets you own. Draw a star next to the other kinds of pets you'd like to own.

Write what these fish are thinking.

Write 5 other words like pet that begin with p and end in t.

p **lan** t
p **o** t
p **i** t
p **or** t
p **lo** t

Page 45

Pets

Would you rather own a dog or a cat? _____

Why? _____

What kind of pet are they?

iguana, snake, turtle **reptiles**

canary, parrot, dove **birds**

rat, gerbil, hamster **rodents**

beagle, lab, hound **dogs**

Raul has 2 kinds of pets: dogs and birds. One day, Raul counted his pets' heads and legs. There were 9 heads and 22 legs. How many dogs and birds does Raul have?

2 dogs

7 birds

Write 1 good thing and 1 bad thing about owning each kind of pet.

Pet	Good thing	Bad thing
Fish		
Hamster		
Parakeet		
Dog		

Page 46

Pets

Each of these 6 children has a different pet. Read the clues. Then write the child's name under his or her pet.
Hint: You will need to read the clues at least 2 times.

| Charlie | Claire | Jack | Kate | Sawyer | Shannon |

• Kate is allergic to dogs.
• Jack's pet does not have legs.
• Shannon's pet lives in a cage.
• Kate's pet has 4 legs.
• Charlie and Sawyer each have a kind of pet that begins with the same letter as their names.

Shannon   Charlie   Jack

Sawyer   Kate   Claire

Page 47

Reptiles

Name _____

Number the reptiles from 1 to 7 according to how dangerous you think they are. The most dangerous one should be number 1.

____ crocodile
____ iguana
____ rattlesnake
____ snapping turtle
____ gecko
____ boa constrictor
____ sea turtle

What reptile did Jim see at the zoo? Read the clues and cross out letters. Then use the leftover letters to write the name of the reptile.

• Cross out the last 2 letters of the alphabet.
• Cross out every letter that is made with exactly 2 straight lines.
• Cross out the letters in Jim's name.

T M V Z
X S E
A N K

Jim saw a __snake__

Would you rather be a crocodile, a boa constrictor, or a sea turtle?

Which one? _____

Why? _____

Page 48

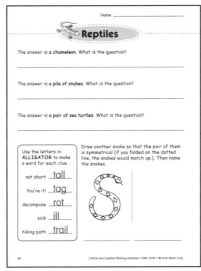

Reptiles

Name _____

The answer is a **chameleon**. What is the question?

_____

The answer is a **pile of snakes**. What is the question?

_____

The answer is a **pair of sea turtles**. What is the question?

_____

Use the letters in **ALLIGATOR** to make a word for each clue.

not short ___tall___
You're it! ___tag___
decompose ___rot___
sick ___ill___
hiking path ___trail___

Draw another snake so that the pair of them is symmetrical (if you folded on the dotted line, the snakes would match up.). Then name the snakes.

Page 49

Reptiles

Name _____

Turn a **lizard** into a **turtle** in just 6 steps. Read each clue and rewrite the word. Change only one letter on each line until you have a **turtle**!

	L	I	Z	A	R	D
Change the 4th letter in the alphabet to the 5th.	L	I	Z	A	R	E
Change the 3rd letter to an R.	L	I	R	A	R	E
Change the letter with just 2 straight lines to a T.	T	I	R	A	R	E
Make the 4th letter the same as the 1st letter.	T	I	R	T	R	E
Make the 5th letter into an L.	T	I	R	T	L	E
Make I into the last vowel in the alphabet.	T	U	R	T	L	E

Page 50

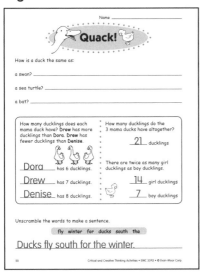

Quack!

Name _____

How is a duck the same as:

a swan? _____
a sea turtle? _____
a bat? _____

How many ducklings does each mama duck have? **Drew** has more ducklings than **Dora**. **Drew** has fewer ducklings than **Denise**.

Dora has 6 ducklings.
Drew has 7 ducklings.
Denise has 8 ducklings.

How many ducklings do the 3 mama ducks have altogether?

___21___ ducklings

There are twice as many girl ducklings as boy ducklings.

___14___ girl ducklings
___7___ boy ducklings

Unscramble the words to make a sentence.

fly winter for ducks south the

__Ducks fly south for the winter.__

Page 51

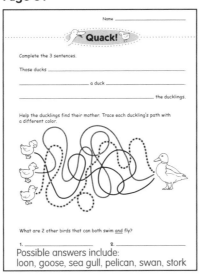

Quack!

Name _____

Complete the 3 sentences.

Those ducks _____

_____ a duck

_____ the ducklings.

Help the ducklings find their mother. Trace each duckling's path with a different color.

What are 2 other birds that can both swim and fly?

1. _____   2. _____

Possible answers include:
loon, goose, sea gull, pelican, swan, stork

Page 52

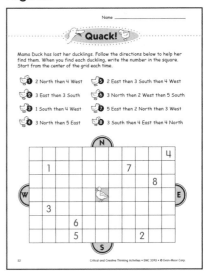

Quack!

Name _____

Mama Duck has lost her ducklings. Follow the directions below to help her find them. When you find each duckling, write the number in the square. Start from the center of the grid each time.

1 2 North then 4 West
2 3 East then 3 South
3 1 South then 4 West
4 3 North then 5 East

5 East then 3 South then 4 West
6 3 North then 2 West then 5 South
7 5 East then 2 North then 3 West
8 3 South then 4 East then 4 North

Page 53

Slugs and Worms

Name _____

How are slugs and worms the same? How are they different? Write 3 ways for each.

Same	Different

Finish these tongue twisters. Use as many words as you can.

Sally Slug saw _____

Willy Worm went _____

Josie lined up 5 worms end to end. Then she lined up 7 slugs the same way. Each worm is 5 inches long, and each slug is 4 inches long. Which line is longer? Circle.

worms   slugs

How much longer? ___3___ inches

If you had to eat either 3 worms or 1 slug, which would you choose?

Why? _____

Page 54

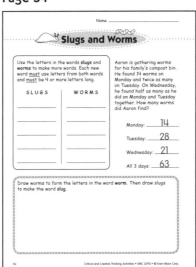

Slugs and Worms

Name _____

Use the letters in the words **slugs** and **worms** to make more words. Each new word must use letters from both words and must be 4 or more letters long.

SLUGS	WORMS

Aaron is gathering worms for his family's compost bin. He found 14 worms on Monday and twice as many on Tuesday. On Wednesday, he found half as many as he did on Monday and Tuesday together. How many worms did Aaron find?

Monday: ___14___
Tuesday: ___28___
Wednesday: ___21___
All 3 days: ___63___

Draw worms to form the letters in the word **worm**. Then draw slugs to make the word **slug**.

Page 55

Slugs and Worms

Name _____

Use the slugs and the worms in the box to make words. Then write the words on the lines. You may use the same slugs and worms more than once.

SP TR BL A E I M
CH ST GR R U

Make up one of your own.

Page 56

Page 57

Analogies

Bee is to sting as mosquito is to **bite**

Bee is to hive as bird is to **nest**

Bee is to yellow as polar bear is to **white**

Bees can sting. What are 3 other animals that can sting?
Possible answers: stingray scorpion, wasp, yellow jacket, jellyfish, some fish

Bees have stripes. What are 3 other animals that have stripes?
Possible answers: zebra, hyena, skunk, bongo, tiger, some fish, some cats, chipmunk

Betty Bee is an odd bee. She will gather nectar only from the flowers with odd-numbered products. Color the correct flowers.

Page 58

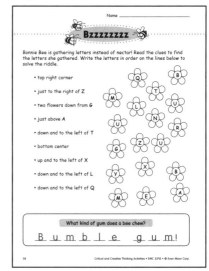

Bonnie Bee is gathering letters instead of nectar! Read the clues to find the letters she gathered. Write the letters in order on the lines below to solve the riddle.

- top right corner
- just to the right of Z
- two flowers down from G
- just above A
- down and to the left of T
- bottom center
- up and to the left of X
- down and to the left of L
- down and to the left of Q

What kind of gum does a bee chew?

B u m b l e   g u m !

Page 59

Page 60

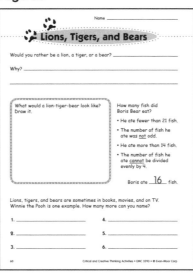

Page 61

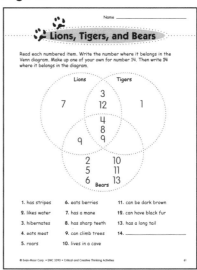

Page 62

Page 63

Page 64

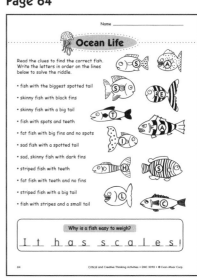

Home Sweet Home

Name _____

Analogies

Picture is to wall as rug is to _floor_

Toilet is to bathroom as oven is to _kitchen_

House is to family as school is to _students_

What is your favorite room in your house? _____

Why? _____

What color is each of these things in your house?	How many of each of these things are in your house?
front door _____	closets _____
refrigerator _____	chairs _____
couch _____	drawers _____
bathroom counter _____	windows _____

Home Sweet Home

Name _____

Cody's family has moved twice, and he has lived in 3 different houses. The green house was not on Maple Street. The blue house was not on Spruce Street. The red house was not on Maple Street or Spruce Street.

What colors were Cody's houses?

Maple Street: _blue_

Spruce Street: _green_

Elm Street: _red_

If you could change one thing about your house, what would it be?

_____

Why? _____

What does this say?

Home   Home
———————
Range

home, home on the range

If there were a fire or a flood at your house and you knew that all of the people and animals were safe, what 3 things would you save?

1. _____
2. _____
3. _____

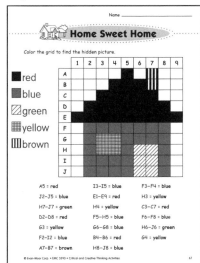

Home Sweet Home

Name _____

Color the grid to find the hidden picture.

■ red
■ blue
▨ green
▦ yellow
▥ brown

(grid A–J rows, 1–9 columns)

A5 = red	I3–I5 = blue	F3–F4 = blue
J2–J5 = blue	E1–E9 = red	H3 = yellow
H7–J7 = green	H4 = yellow	C3–C7 = red
D2–D8 = red	F5–H5 = blue	F6–F8 = blue
G3 = yellow	G6–G8 = blue	H6–J6 = green
F2–I2 = blue	B4–B6 = red	G4 = yellow
A7–B7 = brown	H8–J8 = brown	

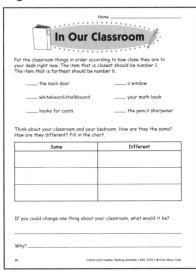

In Our Classroom

Name _____

Put the classroom things in order according to how close they are to your desk right now. The item that is closest should be number 1. The item that is farthest should be number 6.

___ the main door   ___ a window

___ whiteboard/chalkboard   ___ your math book

___ hooks for coats   ___ the pencil sharpener

Think about your classroom and your bedroom. How are they the same? How are they different? Fill in the chart.

Same	Different

If you could change one thing about your classroom, what would it be?

_____

Why? _____

In Our Classroom

Name _____

Name something in your classroom that is:

round _____
sharp _____
soft _____
colorful _____
tiny _____
loud _____

The purpose of a classroom is to provide a place for learning. What are the 5 most important things in your classroom that help you learn?

1. _____
2. _____
3. _____
4. _____
5. _____

If your desk could talk, what would it say? Write it.

Add as many words as you can.

pencil, crayon, chalk, _____

teacher, janitor, nurse, _____

math, spelling, science, _____

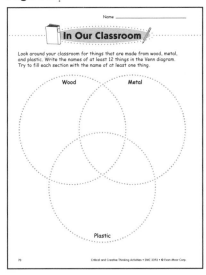

In Our Classroom

Name _____

Look around your classroom for things that are made from wood, metal, and plastic. Write the names of at least 12 things in the Venn diagram. Try to fill each section with the name of at least one thing.

Wood   Metal

Plastic

In the Woods

Name _____

Shh... What can you hear in the woods? Write 3 things.

1. _____ 2. _____ 3. _____

Write a sentence about the woods. Use exactly 7 words.

_____

Forest is another word for **woods**. What are other words for these things you might find in the woods?

rabbit _bunny/hare_

trail _path_

creek _stream_

stone _rock_

twig _stick_

burrow _hole_

You are going for a hike in the woods. Circle the 3 most important things to bring.

compass   book   binoculars

whistle   map   first-aid kit

water   hat   flashlight

bug spray   snack

If you walk 3 miles in an hour, how far will you walk in 90 minutes?

$4\frac{1}{2}$ miles

In the Woods

Name _____

Add 2 more to each list.

raccoon, deer, rabbit, _____, _____

beetle, mosquito, butterfly, _____, _____

Name something in the woods that is...

soft _____
hard _____
rough _____
sharp _____

Draw lines to match the animals with their descriptions. Be careful: You may match only one description to each animal.

woodpecker — nocturnal
squirrel — bushy tail
deer — long ears
raccoon — black and white
rabbit — can fly
owl — eats bugs
skunk — climbs trees
tree frog — brown

What does this say?

A
WO walk ODS

A walk in the woods

In the Woods

Name _____

Use the names of trees to fill in the puzzle. Plan carefully.

(crossword puzzle with answers)

PEACH   SPRUCE   MAPLE
ELM   DOGWOOD   BIRCH
OAK   PALM   WALNUT
CEDAR   HICKORY

3 letters
ASH
ELM
FIR
OAK

4 letters
PALM
~~PINE~~

5 letters
BEECH
BIRCH
CEDAR
MAPLE
PEACH

6 letters
CHERRY
ORANGE
SPRUCE
WALNUT
WILLOW

7 letters
DOGWOOD
HEMLOCK
HICKORY
REDWOOD

Page 74

Name _____

At a Party

The answer is a big party. What is the question?

_____

Write a sentence using the words party, cake, and sister.

_____

_____

Number these things you might do at a party from 1 to 6. The one you like the most should be number 1.

_____ see friends
_____ play games
_____ wear special clothes
_____ meet new people
_____ eat yummy food
_____ see presents opened

Nikki had a lot of balloons at her party.
• There were 3 times as many **red** balloons as **blue** balloons.
• There were 6 more **green** balloons than **blue** balloons.
• There were 14 **green** balloons.

How many balloons of each color were there?

_24_ red balloons
_8_ blue balloons
_14_ green balloons

Page 75

Name _____

At a Party

James is going to a party, but there is something wrong with the directions. Help him find the party by rewriting the directions with the spaces in the correct places.

Dir ecti onst oth ep arty: **Directions to the party:**
Dri venor thdo wnMa inStreet. **Drive north down Main Street.**
Tur nlef tonEl mAve nue. **Turn left on Elm Avenue.**
Dri vef iveb locks. **Drive five blocks.**
Loo kfo rth ere dho us e. **Look for the red house.**
Yo ua reh erel Co meo nin! **You are here! Come on in!**

Analogies
Eat is to cake as ___drink___ is to soda.
Hit is to piñata as ___pin___ is to donkey.
Hokeypokey is to dance as ___(any game)___ is to game.

P is for **party.**
How many p's were on this page before you started to write? _10_

Page 76

Name _____

At a Party

You are throwing a party! Design a cover for the invitation. Then plan what you will need for the party and what your guests will do at the party.

Invitation

Make a list of what you will need for your party.

What will your guests do at the party?

Page 77

Name _____

In the Garden

You can plant 4 things in your garden. What will you plant?

1. _____   3. _____
2. _____   4. _____

Jason planted 12 tomato plants. There are about 15 tomatoes on each of Jason's plants. About how many tomatoes did Jason harvest?

about _180_ tomatoes

What are 3 things that Jason can make with his tomatoes?

1. _____
2. _____
3. _____

Can you think of a vegetable for each of these letters?

S _____
A _____
P _____
C _____
L _____
B _____
R _____
Z _____

Page 78

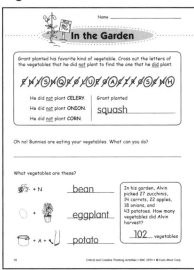

Name _____

In the Garden

Grant planted his favorite kind of vegetable. Cross out the letters of the vegetables that he did not plant to find the one that he did plant.

~~C~~ ~~N~~ ~~Y~~ S ~~M~~ ~~Q~~ ~~R~~ ~~O~~ Q ~~U~~ U ~~P~~ ~~Q~~ A ~~C~~ ~~I~~ ~~I~~ ~~O~~ S ~~E~~ ~~N~~ H

He did not plant CELERY.
He did not plant ONION.
He did not plant CORN.

Grant planted __squash__

Oh no! Bunnies are eating your vegetables. What can you do?

_____

What vegetables are these?

+ N ___bean___
___eggplant___
+ A + ___potato___

In his garden, Alvin picked 27 zucchinis, 14 carrots, 22 apples, 18 onions, and 43 potatoes. How many vegetables did Alvin harvest?

_102_ vegetables

Page 79

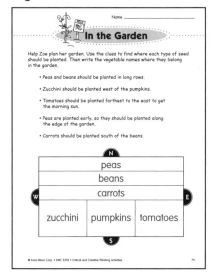

Name _____

In the Garden

Help Zoe plan her garden! Use the clues to find where each type of seed should be planted. Then write the vegetable names where they belong in the garden.

• Peas and beans should be planted in long rows.
• Zucchini should be planted west of the pumpkins.
• Tomatoes should be planted farthest to the east to get the morning sun.
• Peas are planted early, so they should be planted along the edge of the garden.
• Carrots should be planted south of the beans.

N

| peas |
| beans |
| carrots |

W | zucchini | pumpkins | tomatoes | E

S

Page 80

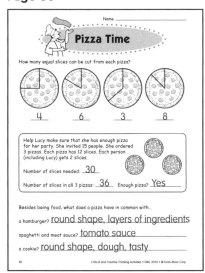

Name _____

Pizza Time

How many equal slices can be cut from each pizza?

_4_   _6_   _3_   _8_

Help Lucy make sure that she has enough pizza for her party. She invited 15 people. She ordered 3 pizzas. Each pizza has 12 slices. Each person (including Lucy) gets 2 slices.

Number of slices needed: _30_
Number of slices in all 3 pizzas: _36_ Enough pizza? _Yes_

Besides being food, what does a pizza have in common with...

a hamburger? _round shape, layers of ingredients_
spaghetti and meat sauce? _tomato sauce_
a cookie? _round shape, dough, tasty_

Page 81

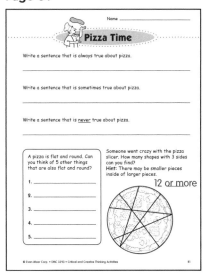

Name _____

Pizza Time

Write a sentence that is always true about pizza.

_____

Write a sentence that is sometimes true about pizza.

_____

Write a sentence that is never true about pizza.

_____

A pizza is flat and round. Can you think of 5 other things that are also flat and round?

1. _____
2. _____
3. _____
4. _____
5. _____

Someone went crazy with the pizza slicer. How many shapes with 3 sides can you find?
Hint: There may be smaller pieces inside of larger pieces.

12 or more

Page 82

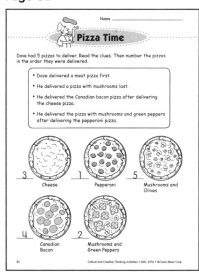

Name _____

Pizza Time

Dave had 5 pizzas to deliver. Read the clues. Then number the pizzas in the order they were delivered.

• Dave delivered a meat pizza first.
• He delivered a pizza with mushrooms last.
• He delivered the Canadian bacon pizza after delivering the cheese pizza.
• He delivered the pizza with mushrooms and green peppers after delivering the pepperoni pizza.

_3_ Cheese   _1_ Pepperoni   _5_ Mushrooms and Olives

_4_ Canadian Bacon   _2_ Mushrooms and Green Peppers

© Evan-Moor Corp. • EMC 3393 • Critical and Creative Thinking Activities

Page 83

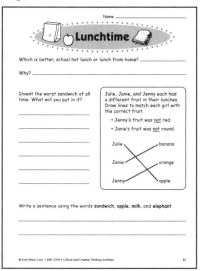

Lunchtime

Which is better, school hot lunch or lunch from home? _____

Why? _____

Invent the worst sandwich of all time. What will you put in it?

_____
_____
_____
_____
_____

Julie, Janie, and Jenny each had a different fruit in their lunches. Draw lines to match each girl with the correct fruit.
• Jenny's fruit was not red.
• Janie's fruit was not round.

Julie — banana
Janie — orange
Jenny — apple

Write a sentence using the words **sandwich, apple, milk,** and **elephant.**

_____
_____

Page 84

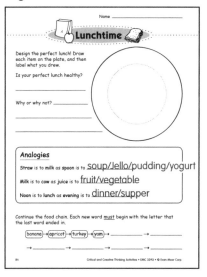

Lunchtime

Design the perfect lunch! Draw each item on the plate, and then label what you drew.

Is your perfect lunch healthy?

_____

Why or why not? _____

Analogies

Straw is to milk as spoon is to soup/Jello/pudding/yogurt

Milk is to cow as juice is to fruit/vegetable

Noon is to lunch as evening is to dinner/supper

Continue the food chain. Each new word must begin with the letter that the last word ended in.

banana → apricot → turkey → yam → _____

_____ → _____ → _____ → _____

Page 85

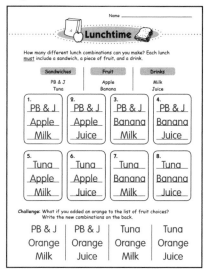

Lunchtime

How many different lunch combinations can you make? Each lunch must include a sandwich, a piece of fruit, and a drink.

Sandwiches	Fruit	Drinks
PB & J	Apple	Milk
Tuna	Banana	Juice

1. PB & J / Apple / Milk
2. PB & J / Apple / Juice
3. PB & J / Banana / Milk
4. PB & J / Banana / Juice
5. Tuna / Apple / Milk
6. Tuna / Apple / Juice
7. Tuna / Banana / Milk
8. Tuna / Banana / Juice

Challenge: What if you added an orange to the list of fruit choices? Write the new combinations on the back.

PB & J	PB & J	Tuna	Tuna
Orange	Orange	Orange	Orange
Milk	Juice	Milk	Juice

Page 86

Eat Your Veggies

There are many kinds of vegetables! Circle the ones you like. Cross off the ones you do not like. Underline the ones you have never tried.

carrots   zucchini   spinach
lettuce   peas   beets
broccoli   asparagus   celery
cucumber   cauliflower   green beans

Draw a star next to the vegetable that you like best.

You are making vegetable soup. What vegetables will you use?

_____
_____
_____
_____
_____

Rachel ate exactly 23 peas from 6 pods. Circle the 6 pods.

One possible combination totaling 23: 2, 3, 3, 4, 5, 6

Page 87

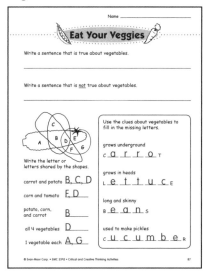

Eat Your Veggies

Write a sentence that is true about vegetables.

_____

Write a sentence that is not true about vegetables.

_____

Write the letter or letters shared by the shapes.

carrot and potato   B, C, D
corn and tomato   F, D
potato, corn, and carrot   B
all 4 vegetables   D
1 vegetable each   A, G

Use the clues about vegetables to fill in the missing letters.

grows underground
c a r r o t

grows in heads
l e t t u c e

long and skinny
b e a n s

used to make pickles
c u c u m b e r

Page 88

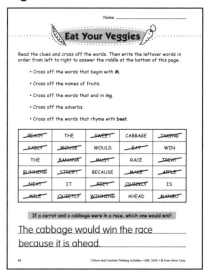

Eat Your Veggies

Read the clues and cross off the words. Then write the leftover words in order from left to right to answer the riddle at the bottom of this page.
• Cross off the words that begin with M.
• Cross off the names of fruits.
• Cross off the words that end in ing.
• Cross off the adverbs.
• Cross off the words that rhyme with beet.

~~PEACH~~	THE	~~SWEET~~	CABBAGE	~~TAKING~~
~~SADLY~~	~~MOUSE~~	WOULD	~~EAT~~	WIN
THE	~~BANANA~~	~~MUST~~	RACE	~~TREAT~~
~~RUNNING~~	~~STREET~~	BECAUSE	~~MAKE~~	~~APPLE~~
~~NEAT~~	IT	~~FEET~~	~~QUICKLY~~	IS
~~MILE~~	~~QUIETLY~~	~~WINNING~~	AHEAD	~~MANGO~~

If a carrot and a cabbage were in a race, which one would win?

The cabbage would win the race because it is ahead.

Page 89

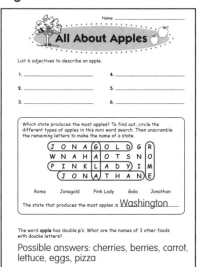

All About Apples

List 6 adjectives to describe an apple.

1. _____   4. _____
2. _____   5. _____
3. _____   6. _____

Which state produces the most apples? To find out, circle the different types of apples in this mini word search. Then unscramble the remaining letters to make the name of a state.

J O N A G O L D G R
W N A H A O T S N O
P I N K L A D Y I M
J O N A T H A N E

Rome   Jonagold   Pink Lady   Gala   Jonathan

The state that produces the most apples is Washington

The word **apple** has double p's. What are the names of 3 other foods with double letters?

Possible answers: cherries, berries, carrot, lettuce, eggs, pizza

Page 90

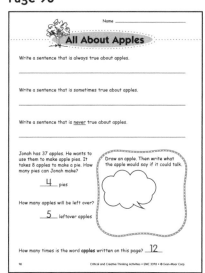

All About Apples

Write a sentence that is always true about apples.

_____

Write a sentence that is sometimes true about apples.

_____

Write a sentence that is never true about apples.

_____

Jonah has 37 apples. He wants to use them to make apple pies. It takes 8 apples to make a pie. How many pies can Jonah make?

4 pies

How many apples will be left over?

5 leftover apples

Draw an apple. Then write what the apple would say if it could talk.

How many times is the word **apples** written on this page? 12

Page 91

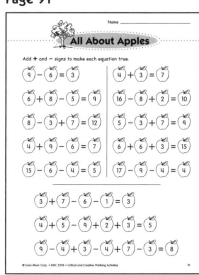

All About Apples

Add + and − signs to make each equation true.

9 − 6 = 3   4 + 3 = 7
6 + 8 − 5 = 9   16 − 8 + 2 = 10
8 − 3 + 7 = 12 5 − 3 + 7 = 9
4 + 9 − 6 = 7   8 + 4 + 3 = 15
15 − 6 − 4 = 5 17 − 9 − 4 = 4

3 + 7 − 6 − 1 = 3
4 + 5 − 9 + 2 + 3 = 5
9 − 4 + 3 − 4 + 7 − 3 = 8

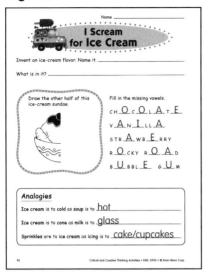

I Scream for Ice Cream

Invent an ice-cream flavor. Name it. _____

What is in it? _____

Draw the other half of this ice-cream sundae.

Fill in the missing vowels.

cH__O__c__O__L__A__t__E
v__A__n__I__ll__A
str__A__wb__E__rry
r__O__cky r__O__A__d
b__U__bbl__E__ g__U__m

Analogies

Ice cream is to cold as soup is to ___hot___

Ice cream is to cone as milk is to ___glass___

Sprinkles are to ice cream as icing is to ___cake/cupcakes___

I Scream for Ice Cream

Ice cream is cold. What are 3 other things that are cold?

1. _____ 2. _____ 3. _____

Ice cream melts. What are 3 other things that melt?

1. _____ 2. _____ 3. _____

Ice cream costs $0.75 per scoop. Sprinkles cost $0.35. How much would each of these cost?

1 scoop with sprinkles ___$1.10___

2 scoops, no sprinkles ___$1.50___

2 scoops with sprinkles ___$1.85___

Mom bought a box of 16 ice-cream bars. Jake and his friends ate half of them. Karla and her friends ate half of what was left. Dad ate 2. How many ice-cream bars are left for Mom?

___2___ ice-cream bars

What are 3 reasons a person might not want to eat ice cream?

1. _____
2. _____
3. _____

I Scream for Ice Cream

Can you think of 21 different flavors of ice cream? Write the name of the flavor on each scoop.

All Wet

What are 10 different things that we use water for?

1. _____ 6. _____
2. _____ 7. _____
3. _____ 8. _____
4. _____ 9. _____
5. _____ 10. _____

Circle raindrops that add up to 16. You may circle as many raindrops as you like. Your circles can overlap. One example is done for you.

How many groups of 16 did you find? _____
___At least 13 groups are possible.___

All Wet

Would you rather take a shower or a bath? _____

Why? _____

Splish-splash! Use the clues to find other words that begin with sp.

where rockets go sp___ace___

to go round and round sp___in___

tipped-over liquid sp___ill___

used to eat soup sp___oon___

to talk sp___eak___

thin pasta sp___aghetti___

Where can you find water in nature?

Unscramble the words to make a sentence.

other rain some come rain away go day again

___Rain rain go away, come again some___
___other day.___

All Wet

The word rain has the letters r and n in it. How many other words can you make that have both of these letters in them? The r must come before the n.
Examples: run, grant

1. _____ 6. _____ 11. _____
2. _____ 7. _____ 12. _____
3. _____ 8. _____ 13. _____
4. _____ 9. _____ 14. _____
5. _____ 10. _____ 15. _____

The word wet has the letters w and t in it. See how many other words you can make that have w and t in them. The w must come before the t.

1. _____ 6. _____ 11. _____
2. _____ 7. _____ 12. _____
3. _____ 8. _____ 13. _____
4. _____ 9. _____ 14. _____
5. _____ 10. _____ 15. _____

What I Wear

Analogies

Sock is to foot as hat is to ___head___

Shirt is to washing machine as dish is to ___dishwasher___

Mitten is to two as glove is to ___five___

Describe the shirt that you are wearing right now. Use as many details as you can. Then draw your shirt in the box.

_____
_____
_____
_____

Grandma knit 3 pairs of socks for each of her grandchildren. She has 14 grandchildren. How many socks did Grandma knit?

___84___ socks

What I Wear

What are 3 reasons you might never wear your favorite shirt again?

1. _____
2. _____
3. _____

Change 1 letter in each word to make a type of clothing.

PARTS ___pants___

SHORT ___shirt___

PRESS ___dress___

LOCK ___sock___

COAL ___coat___

HAM ___hat___

WEST ___vest___

Short-sleeved shirts cost $6. Long-sleeved shirts cost $9. Shannon bought 7 shirts. She spent $51. How many of each type of shirt did Shannon buy?

___4___ short-sleeved shirts

___3___ long-sleeved shirts

What I Wear

You get points for what you are wearing! Use the chart to answer the questions. Show your work.

• How many points are you wearing?

• Compare your points with a friend's.

Who has more points?

How many more points?

How many points do you have altogether?

_____

• Find 2 more people. How many points do all 4 of you have?

• Try to find someone who has the same number of points as you do. Write his or her name.

_____

Item	Points
Shirt	16
Pants or shorts	18
Skirt	18
Dress	15
Socks	6 (each)
Tights or stockings	13
Shoes	7 (each)
Hat	12
Watch	17
Other jewelry	7 (each)
Belt	11
Vest	13
Jacket/sweatshirt	10
Hair clips/bands	14
Braces	19
Glasses	19
Underwear	50

Page 101

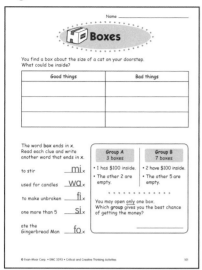

Page 102

Page 103

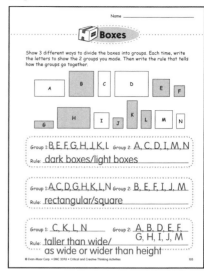

Page 104

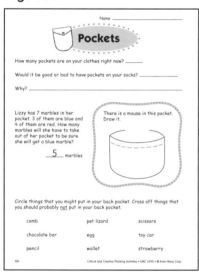

Page 105

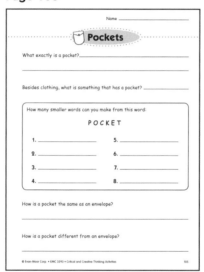

Page 106

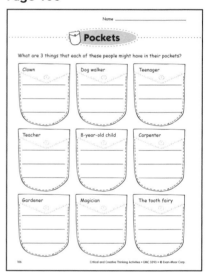

Page 107

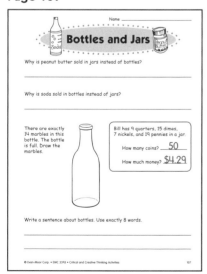

Page 108

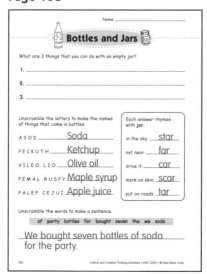

Page 109

Critical and Creative Thinking Activities • EMC 3393 • © Evan-Moor Corp.

Page 110

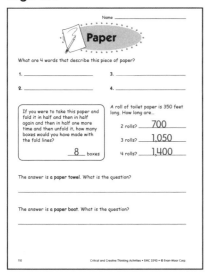

Name _____

Paper

What are 4 words that describe this piece of paper?

1. _____ 3. _____

2. _____ 4. _____

If you were to take this paper and fold it in half and then in half again and then in half one more time and then unfold it, how many boxes would you have made with the fold lines?

8 boxes

A roll of toilet paper is 350 feet long. How long are...

2 rolls? **700**

3 rolls? **1,050**

4 rolls? **1,400**

The answer is a **paper towel**. What is the question?

_____

The answer is a **paper boat**. What is the question?

_____

Page 111

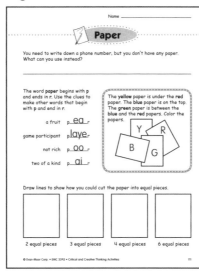

Name _____

Paper

You need to write down a phone number, but you don't have any paper. What can you use instead?

The word **paper** begins with p and ends in r. Use the clues to make other words that begin with p and end in r.

a fruit p_ea_r

game participant p_laye_r

not rich p_oo_r

two of a kind p_ai_r

The **yellow** paper is under the **red** paper. The **blue** paper is on the top. The **green** paper is between the **blue** and the **red** papers. Color the papers.

Draw lines to show how you could cut the paper into equal pieces.

2 equal pieces   3 equal pieces   4 equal pieces   6 equal pieces

Page 112

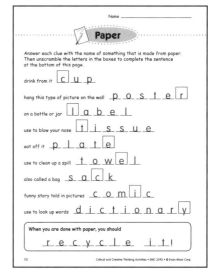

Name _____

Paper

Answer each clue with the name of something that is made from paper. Then unscramble the letters in the boxes to complete the sentence at the bottom of this page.

drink from it c u p

hang this type of picture on the wall p o s t e r

on a bottle or jar l a b e l

use to blow your nose t i s s u e

eat off it p l a t e

use to clean up a spill t o w e l

also called a bag s a c k

funny story told in pictures c o m i c

use to look up words d i c t i o n a r y

When you are done with paper, you should

r e c y c l e   i t!

Page 113

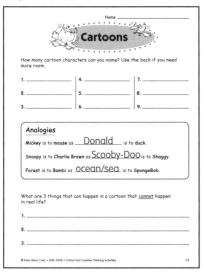

Name _____

Cartoons

How many cartoon characters can you name? Use the back if you need more room.

1. _____ 4. _____ 7. _____

2. _____ 5. _____ 8. _____

3. _____ 6. _____ 9. _____

Analogies

Mickey is to mouse as **Donald** is to duck.

Snoopy is to Charlie Brown as **Scooby-Doo** is to Shaggy.

Forest is to Bambi as **ocean/sea** is to SpongeBob.

What are 3 things that can happen in a cartoon that _cannot_ happen in real life?

1. _____

2. _____

3. _____

Page 114

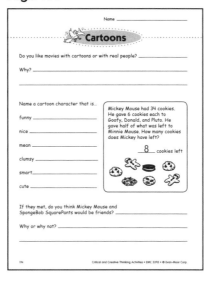

Name _____

Cartoons

Do you like movies with cartoons or with real people? _____

Why? _____

Name a cartoon character that is...

funny _____

nice _____

mean _____

clumsy _____

smart _____

cute _____

Mickey Mouse had 34 cookies. He gave 6 cookies each to Goofy, Donald, and Pluto. He gave half of what was left to Minnie Mouse. How many cookies does Mickey have left?

8 cookies left

If they met, do you think Mickey Mouse and SpongeBob SquarePants would be friends? _____

Why or why not? _____

Page 115

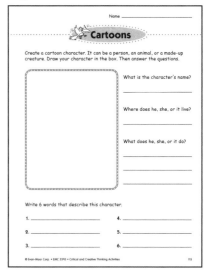

Name _____

Cartoons

Create a cartoon character. It can be a person, an animal, or a made-up creature. Draw your character in the box. Then answer the questions.

What is the character's name?

_____

Where does he, she, or it live?

_____

What does he, she, or it do?

_____

Write 6 words that describe this character.

1. _____ 4. _____

2. _____ 5. _____

3. _____ 6. _____

Page 116

Name _____

Listen!

This is a quiet line.

This line is a little louder.

Draw a really loud line.

The town clock marks the hours with bells—1 chime for 1:00, 2 chimes for 2:00, and so on, until 12:00. How many times altogether will the clock bells chime in 12 hours?

78 chimes

What are 3 things that you would hear...

in a forest? _____

at a ballgame? _____

at a bowling alley? _____

Analogies

Ring is to phone as **honk** is to horn.

Loud is to shout as **quiet** is to whisper.

Clap is to hands as **stomp** is to feet.

Page 117

Name _____

Listen!

What are 3 things that you would _not_ be able to do if you could not hear?

1. _____

2. _____

3. _____

When is it good to whisper, and when is it good to shout?

Whisper	Shout

What is the loudest noise that you can think of? _____

What is the softest noise that you can still hear? _____

What is a sound that you like to hear? _____

What is a sound that you do _not_ like to hear? _____

Page 118

Name _____

Listen!

When a word sounds like what it is describing, it is called **onomatopoeia**. What sounds do the words below describe?

squeak _____

trickle _____

slurp _____

crash _____

pop _____

Write a word that sounds like the description.

a bee _____ a tomato hitting a wall _____

a phone _____ breaking glass _____

a cannon _____ eating an apple _____

a fire _____ horse hooves _____

Write a sentence that uses onomatopoeia.

_____

_____

Page 119

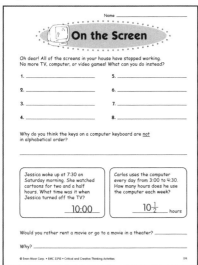

Name _____

On the Screen

Oh dear! All of the screens in your house have stopped working. No more TV, computer, or video games! What can you do instead?

1. _____   5. _____
2. _____   6. _____
3. _____   7. _____
4. _____   8. _____

Why do you think the keys on a computer keyboard are not in alphabetical order?

_____

Jessica woke up at 7:30 on Saturday morning. She watched cartoons for two and a half hours. What time was it when Jessica turned off the TV?

__10:00__

Carlos uses the computer every day from 3:00 to 4:30. How many hours does he use the computer each week?

__10½__ hours

Would you rather rent a movie or go to a movie in a theater?

Why? _____

© Evan-Moor Corp. • EMC 3393 • Critical and Creative Thinking Activities   119

Page 120

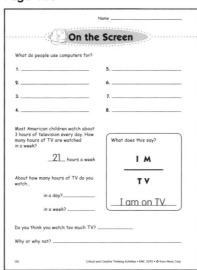

Name _____

On the Screen

What do people use computers for?

1. _____   5. _____
2. _____   6. _____
3. _____   7. _____
4. _____   8. _____

Most American children watch about 3 hours of television every day. How many hours of TV are watched in a week?

__21__ hours a week

About how many hours of TV do you watch...

in a day? _____

in a week? _____

What does this say?

I M
—
T V

I am on TV.

Do you think you watch too much TV? _____

Why or why not? _____

120   Critical and Creative Thinking Activities • EMC 3393 • © Evan-Moor Corp.

Page 121

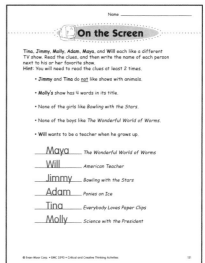

Name _____

On the Screen

Tina, Jimmy, Molly, Adam, Maya, and Will each like a different TV show. Read the clues, and then write the name of each person next to his or her favorite show.
Hint: You will need to read the clues at least 2 times.

• Jimmy and Tina do not like shows with animals.
• Molly's show has 4 words in its title.
• None of the girls like Bowling with the Stars.
• None of the boys like The Wonderful World of Worms.
• Will wants to be a teacher when he grows up.

__Maya__   The Wonderful World of Worms
__Will__   American Teacher
__Jimmy__   Bowling with the Stars
__Adam__   Ponies on Ice
__Tina__   Everybody Loves Paper Clips
__Molly__   Science with the President

© Evan-Moor Corp. • EMC 3393 • Critical and Creative Thinking Activities   121

Page 122

Name _____

Lost and Found

What should you do if you've lost...

your homework? _____

your coat? _____

your dog? _____

Number these things that can be lost from 1 to 6. The one that would be the worst to lose should be number 1.

___ your reading glasses
___ your coat
___ your lunch
___ your pencil
___ the TV remote
___ your pet

Tom, Brian, and Doug each lost something. Brian and Doug did not lose hats. Doug never wears a scarf. Who lost each of these things?

mittens __Doug__
hat __Tom__
scarf __Brian__

What is the most important thing that you have ever lost?

_____

122   Critical and Creative Thinking Activities • EMC 3393 • © Evan-Moor Corp.

Page 123

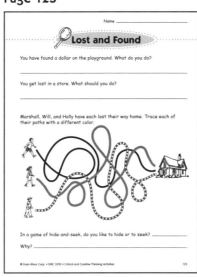

Name _____

Lost and Found

You have found a dollar on the playground. What do you do?

_____

You get lost in a store. What should you do?

_____

Marshall, Will, and Holly have each lost their way home. Trace each of their paths with a different color.

In a game of hide-and-seek, do you like to hide or to seek? _____

Why? _____

© Evan-Moor Corp. • EMC 3393 • Critical and Creative Thinking Activities   123

Page 124

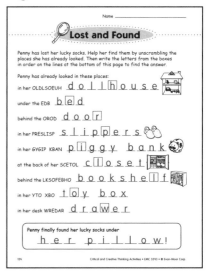

Name _____

Lost and Found

Penny has lost her lucky socks. Help her find them by unscrambling the places she has already looked. Then write the letters from the boxes in order on the lines at the bottom of this page to find the answer.

Penny has already looked in these places:

in her OLDLSOEUH   d o l l h o u s e
under the EDB   b e d
behind the OROD   d o o r
in her PRESLISP   s l i p p e r s
in her GYGIP KBAN   p i g g y b a n k
at the back of her SCETOL   c l o s e t
behind the LKSOFEBHO   b o o k s h e l f
in her YTO XBO   t o y b o x
in her desk WREDAR   d r a w e r

Penny finally found her lucky socks under

h e r p i l l o w !

124   Critical and Creative Thinking Activities • EMC 3393 • © Evan-Moor Corp.

Page 125

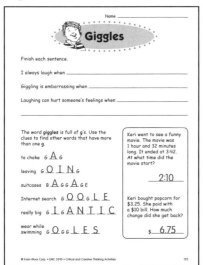

Name _____

Giggles

Finish each sentence.

I always laugh when _____

Giggling is embarrassing when _____

Laughing can hurt someone's feelings when _____

The word giggles is full of g's. Use the clues to find other words that have more than one g.

to choke   G A G
leaving   G O I N G
suitcases   B A G G A G E
Internet search   G O O G L E
really big   G I G A N T I C
wear while swimming   G O G G L E S

Keri went to see a funny movie. The movie was 1 hour and 32 minutes long. It ended at 3:42. At what time did the movie start?

__2:10__

Keri bought popcorn for $3.25. She paid with a $10 bill. How much change did she get back?

$ __6.75__

© Evan-Moor Corp. • EMC 3393 • Critical and Creative Thinking Activities   125

Page 126

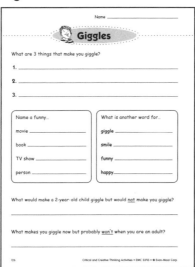

Name _____

Giggles

What are 3 things that make you giggle?

1. _____
2. _____
3. _____

Name a funny...
movie _____
book _____
TV show _____
person _____

What is another word for...
giggle _____
smile _____
funny _____
happy _____

What would make a 2-year-old child giggle but would not make you giggle?

_____

What makes you giggle now but probably won't when you are an adult?

_____

126   Critical and Creative Thinking Activities • EMC 3393 • © Evan-Moor Corp.

Page 127

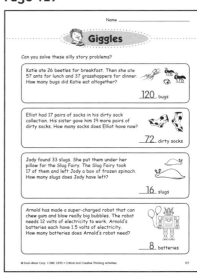

Name _____

Giggles

Can you solve these silly story problems?

Katie ate 26 beetles for breakfast. Then she ate 57 ants for lunch and 37 grasshoppers for dinner. How many bugs did Katie eat altogether?

__120__ bugs

Elliot had 17 pairs of socks in his dirty sock collection. His sister gave him 19 more pairs of dirty socks. How many socks does Elliot have now?

__72__ dirty socks

Jody found 33 slugs. She put them under her pillow for the Slug Fairy. The Slug Fairy took 17 of them and left Jody a box of frozen spinach. How many slugs does Jody have left?

__16__ slugs

Arnold has made a super-charged robot that can chew gum and blow really big bubbles. The robot needs 12 volts of electricity to work. Arnold's batteries each have 1.5 volts of electricity. How many batteries does Arnold's robot need?

__8__ batteries

© Evan-Moor Corp. • EMC 3393 • Critical and Creative Thinking Activities   127

Page 128

Name _____

Nighttime

Analogies

Night is to dark as day is to **light**

Night is to moon as day is to **sun**

Night is to sleep as day is to **wake**

What are 3 things that you can do to help yourself fall asleep?

1. _____
2. _____
3. _____

Each night, Katie reads 8 pages before she goes to sleep. If it takes her 3 minutes to read a page, how long does Katie read each night?

24 minutes

Katie is reading a book that has 92 pages. If she reads 8 pages each night, how many nights will it take Katie to finish the book?

13 nights

128 Critical and Creative Thinking Activities • EMC 3393 • © Evan-Moor Corp.

Page 129

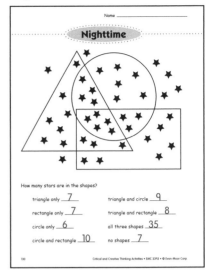

Name _____

Nighttime

What do you think is the perfect bedtime for a child your age? _____

Why? _____
_____

It is nighttime. You are in bed. What do you hear?
_____
_____
_____

Animals that sleep during the day and come out at night are called **nocturnal**. Can you think of 3 nocturnal animals?

1. _____
2. _____
3. _____

What are 3 ways your life would be different if people were nocturnal?

1. _____
2. _____
3. _____

© Evan-Moor Corp. • EMC 3393 • Critical and Creative Thinking Activities 129

Page 130

Name _____

Nighttime

How many stars are in the shapes?

triangle only **7**   triangle and circle **9**

rectangle only **7**   triangle and rectangle **8**

circle only **6**   all three shapes **35**

circle and rectangle **10**   no shapes **7**

130 Critical and Creative Thinking Activities • EMC 3393 • © Evan-Moor Corp.

Page 131

Name _____

My Birthday

When is your birthday?
_____

Do you think it is better to have a birthday in the fall, winter, spring, or summer?
_____

Why? _____

How many months old will you be on your next birthday? Remember, there are 12 months in a year.

_____ months

How many weeks old will you be on your next birthday? Remember, there are 52 weeks in a year.

_____ weeks

Write a sentence about your birthday. Use exactly 8 words.

_____
_____

© Evan-Moor Corp. • EMC 3393 • Critical and Creative Thinking Activities 131

Page 132

Name _____

My Birthday

Fill in the missing vowels for these birthday words.

c**A**k**E**   g**A**m**E**s

pr**E**s**E**nts   **I**c**E** cr**E****A**m

p**A**rty h**A**ts   c**A**ndl**E**s

b**A**ll**OO**ns   **I**nv**I**t**A**t**I****O**ns

How many words can you make with the letters in this word?

BIRTHDAY

1. _____
2. _____
3. _____
4. _____
5. _____
6. _____

This is your birthday cake. Decorate it!

132 Critical and Creative Thinking Activities • EMC 3393 • © Evan-Moor Corp.

Page 133

Name _____

My Birthday

What did Risa get for her birthday? For each clue, find the letter that is in the first boldfaced word but **not** in the second boldfaced word. Then write those letters in order on the lines in the box below to find out what Risa got.

• It is in RE**A**CH but not in CHEER.

• It is in CA**B**LE but not in LACE.

• It is in B**I**TE but not in BEET.

• It is in **C**LOSE but not in LOSER.

• It is in TODA**Y** but not in TOAD.

• It is in RA**C**K but not in RAKE.

• It is in **L**IFT but not in FIGHT.

• It is in TRAD**E** but not in DART.

Risa got

a **b i c y c l e**

What are 3 presents that you would like to get for your birthday?

1. _____ 2. _____ 3. _____

© Evan-Moor Corp. • EMC 3393 • Critical and Creative Thinking Activities 133

Page 134

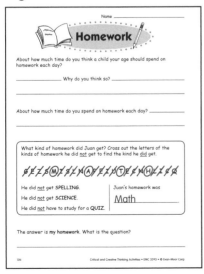

Name _____

Homework

About how much time do you think a child your age should spend on homework each day?

_____ Why do you think so?
_____

About how much time do you spend on homework each day?
_____

What kind of homework did Juan get? Cross out the letters of the kinds of homework he did **not** get to find the kind he **did** get.

He did **not** get SPELLING.

He did **not** get SCIENCE.

He did **not** have to study for a QUIZ.

Juan's homework was

Math

The answer is **my homework**. What is the question?
_____

134 Critical and Creative Thinking Activities • EMC 3393 • © Evan-Moor Corp.

Page 135

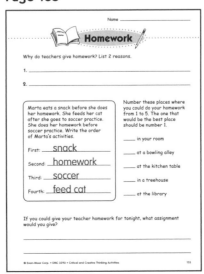

Name _____

Homework

Why do teachers give homework? List 2 reasons.

1. _____
2. _____

Marta eats a snack before she does her homework. She feeds her cat after she goes to soccer practice. She does her homework before soccer practice. Write the order of Marta's activities.

First: **snack**

Second: **homework**

Third: **soccer**

Fourth: **feed cat**

Number these places where you could do your homework from 1 to 5. The one that would be the best place should be number 1.

____ in your room

____ at a bowling alley

____ at the kitchen table

____ in a treehouse

____ at the library

If you could give your teacher homework for tonight, what assignment would you give?
_____

© Evan-Moor Corp. • EMC 3393 • Critical and Creative Thinking Activities 135

Page 136

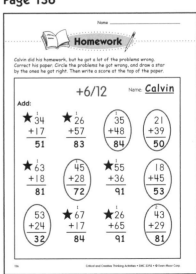

Name _____

Homework

Calvin did his homework, but he got a lot of the problems wrong. Correct his paper. Circle the problems he got wrong, and draw a star by the ones he got right. Then write a score at the top of the paper.

+6/12   Name: **Calvin**

Add:

★ 34 +17 = 51   ★ 26 +57 = 83   35 +48 = 84   21 +39 = 50

★ 63 +18 = 81   45 +28 = 72   ★ 55 +36 = 91   18 +45 = 53

53 +24 = 32   ★ 67 +17 = 84   ★ 26 +65 = 91   43 +29 = 81

136 Critical and Creative Thinking Activities • EMC 3393 • © Evan-Moor Corp.

Page 137

Name _____

Books

Do you like to read? _____

Why or why not? _____

Think about the books that you have read or have had read to you. Which one was the...

funniest? _____

scariest? _____

longest? _____

Taylor got 12 books from the library. One-third of them were about birds. One-fourth of them were about cats. The rest were about monkeys. How many of the books were about monkeys?

_5_ monkey books

Which kinds of books have you read? Write R for the ones you have read. Write N for the ones you have not read.

____ chapter books   ____ science books

____ picture books   ____ manga

____ comic books   ____ joke books

____ animal books   ____ fantasy books

____ biographies   ____ nonfiction books

© Evan-Moor Corp. • EMC 3393 • Critical and Creative Thinking Activities   137

Page 138

Name _____

Books

How are a bookstore and a library the same and different? List 3 ways for each.

Same	Different

What is the name of the last book that you read? _____

Write a fact about the last book that you read.

_____

Write an opinion about the last book that you read.

_____

Analogies

Book is to shelf as sock is to **drawer/dresser**

Book is to read as music is to **listen/hear**

Book is to author as painting is to **artist/painter**

138   Critical and Creative Thinking Activities • EMC 3393 • © Evan-Moor Corp.

Page 139

Name _____

Books

Each of these 6 children is reading a different book. Read the clues. Then write the child's name next to his or her book.
Hint: You will need to read the clues at least 2 times.

- **Meredith** and **Ramon** both chose books about dogs.
- **Christina** will need special materials in order to use her book.
- **George's** book is about mythical creatures.
- **Derek's** book is not about animals.
- None of the girls chose a book with the number 101 in the title.

Meredith
George
Izzie
Ramon
Christina
Derek

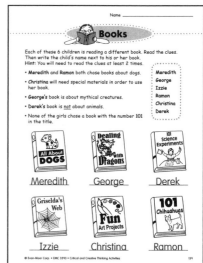

Meredith   George   Derek

Izzie   Christina   Ramon

© Evan-Moor Corp. • EMC 3393 • Critical and Creative Thinking Activities   139

Page 140

Name _____

Cents Sense

The answer is a **quarter**. What is the question?

_____

The answer is **two nickels**. What is the question?

_____

Would you rather have:

22 nickels or ~~12 dimes~~?

~~22 nickels~~ or 5 quarters?

~~15 dimes~~ or 5 quarters?

Write cent, sent, or scent.

a letter   **sent**

a flower   **scent**

a penny   **cent**

Put these coins in order from the oldest to the newest.

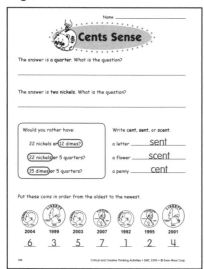

2004	1999	2003	2007	1992	1995	2001
6	3	5	7	1	2	4

140   Critical and Creative Thinking Activities • EMC 3393 • © Evan-Moor Corp.

Page 141

Name _____

Cents Sense

Pretend that you have 1,000 pennies. What are 3 things that you could do with them besides spending them?

1. _____

2. _____

3. _____

Analogies

Quarter is to circle as dollar bill is to **rectangle**

Dime is to silver as penny is to **copper**

Penny is to 1¢ as nickel is to **5¢**

A new $0.75 coin is being made. You get to design it!

Who will be on the front? _____

What will be on the back? _____

Draw the two sides of the new coin.

◯ ◯

What will the coin be called? _____

© Evan-Moor Corp. • EMC 3393 • Critical and Creative Thinking Activities   141

Page 142

Name _____

Cents Sense

Each piggy bank shows the amount of money and the number of coins that are inside. Use letters to tell which coins are in each piggy bank.
Hint: You may want to use real coins.

P = Penny
N = Nickel
D = Dime
Q = Quarter

$0.17
5 coins
NNNPP

$0.33
7 coins
DDNNPPP

$0.61
6 coins
QDDDNP

$0.90
8 coins
QDDDDDNNN

142   Critical and Creative Thinking Activities • EMC 3393 • © Evan-Moor Corp.